Garry Schofi

Season's Diary 1992-3

Garry Schofield's
Season's Diary 1992-3

Garry Schofield
in association with Phil Caplan

The Pentland Press Limited
Edinburgh • Cambridge • Durham

First published in 1993 by
The Pentland Press Ltd.
1 Hutton Close
South Church
Bishop Auckland
Durham

ISBN 1 85821 098 4

Typeset by CBS, Felixstowe, Suffolk
Printed and bound by Antony Rowe Ltd., Chippenham

*To all those who have inspired,
believed in and encouraged
by their words and deeds*

CONTENTS

ILLUSTRATIONS

Acknowledgements

To those who generously supplied their
pictures and gave permission for their
reproduction and to copy typist Ros Caplan
for her continued patience and effort.

Foreword

As one of the biggest names in the Rugby League world, life is rarely dull for Garry Schofield and the 1992/93 season was no exception for a variety of reasons.

As the code becomes increasingly newsworthy at national level, star players find themselves in the spotlight far more and have to cope with new pressures.

Garry Schofield returned from the 1992 tour as great Britain captain, having had the immense satisfaction of leading the side to a record Test win over the Kangaroos in Melbourne and a series triumph in New Zealand.

There was no time to rest on his laurels for the English season included the honour and major test of being skipper of Great Britain in the World Cup Final against Australia at Wembley and seeking to be part of the Leeds revival in a new-look team.

It all meant he could never relax and his performances were subject to the closest scrutiny, nor did the season go according to script.

Schofield found himself on a roller-coaster, either earning high praise for a Leeds victory or in some cases blame for a defeat and there were too many of the latter to satisfy their long-suffering fans.

Among the highs was a hat-trick of tries in leading Britain to an overwhelming victory in France but he missed the return on his home ground of Headingley because of a suspension imposed by his club – very much a rarity.

He was also a member of the Leeds team which suffered a club record Challenge Cup defeat and that in the semi-final as Widnes continued to maintain their stranglehold over the Headingley men in big matches.

Leeds continued to be on the outside looking in as another season without a trophy ticked by.

Off the field Schofield was very much part of the effort to keep the Leeds club in the public eye and he faced a full calendar of events.

His diary of a mixed and sometimes traumatic season gives an intriguing insight into the life and times of a star player. As he discovered, by no means for the first time, there are no half-measures in top-class professional sport these days.

Trevor Watson.

Chapter One

Reflections and Aspirations

The long plane journey back from the Antipodes following the end of the 1992 Tour allowed time for quiet contemplation and assessment. Whilst the two Tests in New Zealand had been their traditional, uncompromising confrontations, from which a tired British party had ultimately emerged victorious, it was the Australians who were at the forefront of my thoughts.

In retrospect, although it was disappointing not to win the Ashes and again be so near and yet so far from success, we did achieve a tremendous amount. Even before we went out there the critics had been writing us off saying we had taken on too hard an itinerary by agreeing to play against Winfield Cup teams, but the midweek side managed to remain unbeaten which was a great credit to them and an indication of the way the English League had picked itself up over the previous three or four seasons. The last touring side that went there in 1988 would not have had much of a chance if faced with the same sort of challenge, but we were at last starting to see the rewards of a more professional approach spreading throughout the game. Our standards of play had undoubtedly improved and it was a major surprise to ourselves as much as anybody that we could now compete consistently at the highest levels.

In the Test series, playing under the pressure of trying to win back the

Ashes after twenty-two years, we performed highly creditably. In the First Test it was disappointing not to turn our early chances into tries and we knew that the final score of 22-6 was in no way a reflection of the difference between the two teams, and that the Aussies were there for the taking. The Second Test will always remain in my mind as an undoubted career highlight and stay in the memory of everyone who played and was at Melbourne that historic night. Our 33-10 victory proved what we already knew, that the Australians were only human and if you pressurise them they come up with mistakes just like everyone else. The last Test turned out to be something of an anticlimax, with the game coming a week too early for us. In the English League we still do not play pressurised football week in and week out and if we could have played that Test a week later then we could have settled ourselves down a little and prepared better for it. In the end, however, we did not do ourselves justice with our performance and the Australians were the better team on the night and ran out worthy winners and deserved to take the series. All in all though, it was a good tour for me personally, achieving an ambition of leading Great Britain in the quest for the Ashes, and realistically for the game as a whole. Fresh on the horizon was the opportunity for instant revenge in the World Cup Final and for both the team and management that match could not come quickly enough.

Perhaps, unlike some of the others, I was not physically shattered at the end of it, having been used to playing back-to-back football, but mentally there was always going to be a challenge preparing for another big English season. We came back towards the end of July, just six weeks prior to the start and with Leeds already in the midst of exhaustive pre-season training. For me the priority was to get a break from rugby to recharge my enthusiasm, spend some time with the family and generally relax. I returned to Headingley, completely refreshed, a fortnight before the kick-off and in those four weeks away my only contact with sport had been in attempting to unmask the vagaries of golf. To try and use touring to

2

explain ineffective performances at the start of a season is a pretty poor excuse.

The new campaign was always going to start with added spice for me as I had turned down an approach from Hull at the start of the summer to return as player-coach. I spoke to their chairman, Stephen Watson, who proposed the idea and I did not immediately reject it out of hand. I took some time to think about the implications even before any sort of terms were discussed and although it was an interesting offer, realistically at that time in my career I was not ready to take on such a level of responsibility, especially going to board meetings every other week. Irrespective of any other considerations there were always going to be two major stumbling blocks, the transfer fee if Leeds had released me, which I did not think they would have, and the accompanying contract payments. The talks only lasted two or three days and I suppose the deal was never really on but it was nice to be appreciated back at the Boulevard, especially as everybody knows I am not the most popular person when I go back there to play. It also came as a great surprise, particularly as the previous two Hull coaches had been recruited from Australia, but I still felt that I had a few good years left in me and a lot to offer playing at the top level, although coaching and management remain a future ambition and something which you have to start thinking about and planning for at some stage.

For Leeds, the real preparations for the new season began late because of the stagnancy of the transfer market. Following the side's collapse at the end of the previous season, recruitment of top class players to expand the squad had become even more of a priority as manager Doug Laughton tried to build his own team around him rather than rely on what he had inherited. Our priorities were two forwards and, following Bobby Goulding's well-publicised disciplinary misdemeanour on a pre-season trip when it became obvious that he would be leaving the club, a scrum half. Doug did ask me about several players who might have been available, but as is inevitable at a club the size and profile of Leeds,

3

rumours and speculation continually abounded. Doug did approach Deryck Fox and Andy Gregory and managed to recruit Andy, a great player who he felt could bring out the best of the squad in the short term and pass on his knowledge to talented youngster, Gareth Stephens. The signing of Gary Mercer, one of the world's finest, hardest and most respected second rowers was just what we needed, but we still missed out on a top line front rower, someone who could impose themselves on other teams and dominate their opposite number when the time came to stand up and be counted. The ideal man would have been Andy Platt, who again proved consistently and conclusively on the tour that he was the best in the world. He returned out of contract at Wigan and could not seem to agree terms. Leeds did make an approach but once Wigan had been comprehensively defeated by Saint Helens in the Charity Shield they realised they had to keep him. Alternatively, I believed Lee Crooks would have done an excellent job for us but unfortunately Leeds do not re-sign players who have left the club. With the capture of Mick Worrall and Andy Goodway, Doug picked up two experienced second rowers who he thought could do specific jobs at Leeds.

As I had been either touring (in '84, '88, '90, and '92) or in the Australian League (for Balmain in '85, '86, and '87 and Wests in '89) over the previous eight summers, I had never really done a full pre-season training regime. Leeds began in June with a series of heavy weight sessions three or four times a week for three or four weeks before starting a programme of long distance running consisting of five mile treks three times a week, which fortunately I missed! Allied to that, strict emphasis is now placed on personal fitness programmes, specialised to suit individual requirements and also on a controlled diet and nutritional intake. This has become increasingly important and is something that again has been instigated by the Australians and is now starting to filter through our game from the top level. They set the trend with the tour of their "Invincibles" in '82 and we had to reshape our game at all strata, including every aspect of preparation in order to compete. Instead of relying on our traditional fare of fish and chips, meat pies, kebabs and burgers, we are carefully monitored on a balanced diet of carbohydrates, proteins and vitamins, such as pasta, chicken, fish and fruit. Not only does that make a dent in the weekly shopping bill but it also forces further sacrifices on the part of the family. Crucially, a healthy diet is not just important for maintaining energy levels, but also for building bodily resistance for injury prevention and recovery. It also extends to all meals, with the Great Britain management faxing clubs with suggested menus for their players, including muesli for breakfast and fruit instead of lunch. It is all part of a totally professional approach to the demands of the sport.

In the final couple of weeks prior to the start of the season, as the new signings started to arrive, squad training sessions began to take on a greater intensity and relevance. The responsibilities for organising the side on the pitch became apparent and centred crucially around myself and Andy Gregory as the key half-backs. The modern game also demands a balanced pack with two prop forwards who are going to do the donkey work of taking the ball up all day and making the hard yardage. The second row needs to include a defender and a penetrative wide out runner, and one will be expected to compensate and cover for the other in their specialised roles. That releases a loose forward like Ellery Hanley who can then be given a roving commission out wide to pick up the pieces. The half-backs become the linchpins for releasing the centres and wingers, an area of the team where Doug had realised the need for greater pace, strength and direct running and had prompted his signings of first the classy ex-All Black, Craig Innes, and, during the early part of the summer, Bath winger, Jim Fallon. The acquisition of Great Britain full back Alan Tait was important in giving the side confidence from a reliable last line of defence combined with the threat of genuine pace linking up from the back. Despite the late signing of Andy Gregory, we envisaged no problem in settling into complementary patterns of play, having admired each other's games

5

whilst playing together for Great Britain. The scrum-half will tend to organise the forwards forty to forty-five yards out from our own line, and then, once that territorial position has been maintained, the stand-off's responsibility is to create the space to get the back line moving and playing free flowing rugby, which has always been the Leeds tradition. Nowadays, however, it has become increasingly necessary to consolidate some of the flair because of the pressure generated by the improved coaching of defences. This innovation has placed a greater emphasis on the disciplined need to hit the ball up and provide a tight kick-and-chase game to clear your lines. Teams can no longer afford to lose the ball near their own line when playing the calibre of the top First Division sides, whose finishing is becoming increasingly lethal. The game plan now includes the need to sacrifice the unorthodox for patience on some occasions and this is constantly reinforced throughout regular and pre-season training sessions.

With the mounting expectation and anticipation of things on the pitch, I was conscious of maintaining and cultivating the interest surrounding me off the field, a process that had started when I took over the mantle of the Great Britain captaincy. As a sportsman I fervently believe that you have to put something back into the game and let people know what is going on and how you feel about it. The chance to write a newspaper column for *Yorkshire on Sunday* and appear regularly on *Boots 'n All* not only added interest and a new dimension to the issues of the season but offered the opportunity of a new career direction after the playing days are over. What is more, I do genuinely enjoy it and the people I work for seem to think I do a reasonable job. I have always tried to base my opinions and comments on a central tenet of honesty and I have never been a person to make excuses or run away from the truth. If you are beaten by the better side I have always believed in coming out and saying so rather than mulling over "if onlys". More important is to work for the chance of revenge next time round. Even though I had been at the peak of the sport during the summer, the new impending season signalled renewed ambition, aims and targets.

Despite having been in the game for nine seasons I had yet to win a major domestic trophy, having lost in one Challenge Cup and three Regal Trophy finals. The big one in all players' minds is Wembley, but heading towards the opening league encounter against Saint Helens we all knew that opposing sides were not going to lie down for us. Because Leeds are a big, high profile club yet to fulfil their true potential teams coming to Headingley in particular have always managed to raise their game accordingly. The reason might be envy, not necessarily of the team but certainly because we have got the best facilities in the League, especially for the players. Nevertheless, if we do not go out and do it on the park having such a set-up is all a bit of a waste of time. Once again, with so many people waiting for and almost willing us to fail, we were not short of motivation or desire.

Chapter Two

Let Battle Commence

Saint Helens (Home) - Stones Bitter Championship 31/8/92

Yet again the fixture computer had shown us few favours. The previous year "fate" had sent us back to Dougie's old haunt, Widnes, whilst to start this season we had been drawn to take on The Saints at Headingley. The prospect of a large Bank Holiday crowd and bumper pay-day was tempered by the realisation that they were not the opposition we would have picked given the choice, especially with a side who had yet to really get to know each other's style of play. Additionally, we were at a distinct disadvantage having not had a pre-season game to test out our fitness and strategy. We were supposed to have played Castleford but they had been drawn in the preliminary round of the Yorkshire Cup, a match had been arranged at Scarborough before their swift and sad demise, and agreement reached to travel to Blackpool to help relaunch and celebrate their return to the town only to find that they did not have a ground ready. The game against Saints, traditionally one of the fastest and most attractive fixtures of the season, had looked even more of a daunting task, especially as they had already played four competitive games by then including the full-blooded Charity Shield encounter with Wigan which they had won easily.

We went into the game optimistic of getting a result, especially looking round the dressing-room at the talents that had been brought together, but by the same token, we knew that if we competed but did not win that it would not be the end of the world or a pointer to the final outcome at the end of the season. There was a certain vibrancy within the squad matched by a resolve and determination as the kick-off approached. Contrary to what a lot of people may think, Dougie does not say a lot in his team talks. He prefers to be more of an individual man manager and tactition, picking out one or two key individuals or specific ploys used by the opposition and pin-pointing the elements worked on in our own game plan during practice in pre-season training. We knew to expect an open, flowing game with Saint Helens' commitment to keen support play and keeping the ball alive. Fortunately, I have never suffered from nerves, only a sense of keen expectation coupled with the realisation that as soon as the gum shield is in then it is time to go to work.

That opening match marked my third season at stand-off and I have consciously altered my game and style of play to accommodate the different responsibilities and demands required in that role. It is no longer important to set myself a try target despite having gained the reputation of being something of a poacher when I played in the centre. That aspect had been a major goal, but now I am primarily an organiser and provider, looking to create chances and set up tries for others. If I do manage to get on the scoresheet now and then I look on it as something of a bonus. That is not to say that I have lost the thrill or enjoyment of crossing the whitewash, especially if it comes from a planned move. That was not, however, the case in the first half against Saints when I went in from a neat Andy Gregory pass to level the game up. Really, I should not have been in that move. In theory Greg takes it to the blind side and tries to pick up one of the second rowers out wide, but the defence brought the dummy and I just happened to be standing on the inside as the gap opened up four or five yards out from the line, which is my sort of distance, and I gratefully dived over.

Although Saints had come out well primed as we had expected and managed to take a half time lead, we knew that we had started effectively and could hold our own with them, especially if we came up with an early strike in the second half. Ellery managed that after I had dropped him off a short ball to split the cover and at 12-11 up the game was there for the taking. Unfortunately, as became symptomatic of our start to the season as a whole, a series of silly, self-inflicted schoolboy errors turned the initiative over to Saints and their ruthless exploitation of them as they got stronger in the latter stages gave them the final advantage. Nevertheless, there were some promising signs for the team from that performance and I felt especially happy with my defensive contribution. That is probably the part of my game that I have consciously worked on the most and the hardest since being switched to stand off. I realised early on that I had to up my work rate on defence and that can only be achieved by putting in hard work on your own on the weights and in the gymnasium. Out in the centre, being further away from the action the emphasis is more on man-to-man marking and explosive running, whereas being involved in the middle of the action I knew that I would now have to make twenty to twenty-five tackles a match frequently on front and second row forwards and that bulking up would be essential.

The immediate reaction in the dressing-room afterwards was one of inevitable disappointment and contemplation. The standard of the First Division nowadays is such that to challenge realistically for the Championship Title you cannot afford to lose your home games, irrespective of the opposition. Even though there are no easy games we certainly could have done without facing a confident Saints side so early on, but despite the mistakes that continually put us under pressure, we all tried to stress the more positive aspects of our play which we could build on. Undoubtedly the most significant blow was the injury to Gary Mercer on his début, which had left him with a jaw broken in two places following an accidental

11

collision in the tackle. At the time it happened we did not think it was too serious but as the diagnosis became apparent we realised the severe implications it would have on a limited squad. His projected eight week absence was always likely to expose the lack of strength in depth in the "A" team. The confidence and spirit of the side had not been adversely affected by the result, it was not a matter of picking ourselves up for the testing trip to Halifax, we knew what we were capable of once the débutants had settled in, even if we did not have the precious commodity of time on our side. We were looking forward to the trip to Thrum Hall to face a side that was also in the process of reshaping itself following some big name summer signings.

Before that I made a highly enjoyable Monday night début on *Boots 'n All* to discuss the weekend's events and inevitably faced the stick meted out by Eddie and Stevo, something that I was to become increasingly used to. I felt comfortable under the glare of the studio lights with the cameras on me, whilst experiencing the new and strange sensation of wearing make-up, a fashion for which rugby players are not usually noted. As a representative of the biggest club in the League I soon realised that I was there to be knocked down if we did not come up with the right results. Far from being a distraction from the main job in hand the media work not only provides welcome light relief in a relaxed atmosphere even when discussing the most contentious of issues, but it also allows me to see the game from an alternative perspective. Without that kind of outlet and outside interests plus the odd game of golf I would probably immerse myself in my profession twenty-four hours a day and it would drive me insane.

Much had been made of the instigation of full-time training, commitment and professionalism at Leeds for the start of the season in an effort to match and combat the great strides made in that direction at Wigan, a factor that most analysts regarded as the key to their continued dominance. The major difference in terms of team preparation is that it enables the

12

club to bring the players in fresh during the day rather than after work at night. A weekly training programme had been devised amongst the backroom staff to cover all aspects of mental and physical application.

On Mondays, which previously had been a rest day to recover from the bruises from the match the day before, the squad now goes swimming at around eleven o'clock for an hour or so. The programme in the pool typically consists of seven to eight lengths, followed by diving and relay competitions. About eight to ten of the squad based in Yorkshire meet at the International Pool in Leeds whilst the same practice goes on for the Lancashire based lads across the Pennines. Tuesday's training consists primarily of fitness work and stamina running without any ball work, illustrating the importance now attached to that aspect of the game and the need for the players to be high class athletes. Wednesday is more of an individual session determined by what the fitness coach, in this case Kiwi Dean Riddle, who was another of Dougie's influential summer signings, assesses that each player needs. This follows on from the personal plans he set during the pre-season to monitor skills and fitness levels and may range from sprint work or weights to improving and developing a kicking game. The emphasis on Thursday switches to sprint work and ball work, and that is maintained during Friday's session where game-related ball drills are the priority activity. Saturday is usually kept as a rest day to prepare for Sunday's game, although specialist injury treatment and rehabilitation exercises are available as necessary throughout the week. The club also puts on food for the players to maintain and monitor the strict and healthy dietary controls necessary for putting back into the body the right constituents that training has taken out.

Prior to the Halifax game, Leeds announced the major signing of Kevin Iro on a long term contract signalling his return to the English game from Manly. As soon as Doug became aware of his availability he moved in to sign him, much to the surprise of Bob Lindner who, like Deryck Fox before him, had thought he was on his way to wearing a blue and amber shirt. Kevin's impending arrival, prior to the full extent of his ankle injury being known, provided a massive boost to the squad's morale. We realised that defensively we were a little lax on the right hand side, with due respect to Carl Gibson who would be the first to admit that he is more effective as an out and out winger, and Kevin's presence was expected to fill that void more than adequately.

Despite the fact that we hold regular team meetings, most often on a Tuesday to assess the strengths and weaknesses of our performance the week before, we do not hold a briefing on the opposition. Dougie is far more concerned with perfecting our own performance and in many cases we are not even sure of the final line-up of our adversaries until we run out to meet them on the pitch on the Sunday afternoon. His philosophy is to let them concern themselves with us rather than us worry about them.

Halifax (Away) - Stones Bitter Championship 6/9/92

If the meeting with Saint Helens had, realistically, come too early, I had to admit that the prospect of playing at Thrum Hall on a nice, balmy September afternoon rather than in the midst of inhospitable winter made a pleasant change. We are spoilt at Headingley by the spaciousness of our dressing-rooms, especially when compared to places like Halifax where it is often no joke trying to cram fifteen blokes the size of rugby players into a confined area. The pitch was nicely grassed this time, unlike in January or February when it is rock hard, invariably caused by a freezing wind blowing off the top of the Pennines and adding to the already intimidatory atmosphere created by having six or seven thousand fanatical home 'speckies' on your back and very close to you. That combination of intense cold and fervour can be off-putting at the best of times, but it is a nice, close, traditional ground that can generate a great genuine occasion. It is certainly easy to hear the inevitable taunting on the pitch which, even by this early stage, was primarily centred around chants of "What a waste of money!" That kind of humour is accepted as part and parcel of the game and as much a spur as a slur, it is only when at certain places the content turns personal and hurtful that it can start to upset although hopefully not affect you.

An additional pressure for me as we looked to put the season back on the rails was to inherit the goal kicking after John Gallagher had been omitted from the side. A reliable kicker like Frano Botica for example, can add an extra dimension to his side's confidence if they know that just about every time they score anywhere on the park it is probably going to be worth six points. I took the job on initially mainly by default and was less than successful, leading to Colin Maskill having a go at it until he was injured. The game itself was again characterised by our own basic errors that threw away a winning situation after we had weathered the expected storm early on. With the score line finely balanced into the second half and beginning to gain the ascendancy we made enough clear chances to take the spoils. Perhaps the most significant turning point of the game was when I had a try disallowed for a foot in touch after an exhausting sixty yards run. At first I was annoyed because I was certain that I had got the ball down fairly but when I saw the incident again on the replays on Sky it did show that I had been caught by David Cooper and slid my right leg into touch before grounding the ball. In this case the touch judge made the right decision when called upon, and if I had seen him after reviewing it I would have apologised. A score at that time would have given us the lead and the confidence to complete the job by taking the game to Halifax but they realised that they were still in it, that we had again failed to turn our spell of dominance into points and they upped their tempo, began to take their chances and never looked back.

The loss of Andy Gregory halfway through the second half with what turned out to be a major knee injury was a severe blow to our organisation, especially as we did not have a back replacement on the bench. I had to switch to scrum half with Ellery at stand-off, and we never recovered from having to make that reshuffle. The way we dropped off in the last fifteen minutes and conceded farcical tries was particularly disturbing and something for which there was no excuse or reason. It certainly was not lack of fitness in only our second game after a strenuous pre-season training programme and may well have been born out of mounting frustration that things were not working. In contrast Halifax had visibly seemed to grow in confidence as we put the pressure on ourselves and ended up beating us by a wider margin than we would have hoped.

One aspect of this match, along with several others as it would turn out, was the confrontation with ex-players who had recently left the club, most notably John Bentley on his try scoring début and Gary Divorty, who both had very big games. It is true that players turning out against their old club perform as if they have got a point to prove and invariably play above themselves, but there is never any animosity and often great pleasure in seeing old friends continuing to thrive in the game.

After the match we were annoyed that we had yet again let slip a match that we could have won, especially as both games had been televised and we had given the pundits, some of whom relished our demise, all the ammunition they needed. With barely a fortnight gone plenty of people were predicting a long hard season for us. Constant talk of "crisis" was certainly premature but there was little doubt that if the knives were not out then they had certainly been sharpened. Rumours abounded about unrest at the club for various reasons which was only to be expected. If people are talking sense or want realistic analysis then you do not mind discussing it with them, whether it is after the game, back at Headingley or if we have gone our separate ways and are recognised socially. I would be happy talking to people about the game twenty-four hours a day, but if all they want to do is slag off the club, me or my fellow professionals, then it is time to walk away.

With the spotlight then very much on Leeds, my attentions turned to Australia and in particular the unexpected chance to become involved in the Winfield Cup again during the 1993 off-season. Manly spoke directly to my agent to see if I would be interested in joining them. Initially I was not keen on the idea because of the rarefied, pressurised atmosphere surrounding the game in Sydney. No sooner have you come off the pitch on Sunday than you are preparing for and thinking about the next encounter the following week and with all the media hype and attention it is literally a seven days a week occupation over there. I like to relax a bit, especially straight after the game and until the next formal training session on the Tuesday. When I considered that it was Manly and knowing their coach Graham Lowe quite well, a man for whom I have a lot of respect both on and off the pitch, I decided to investigate their terms further, see what the offer included by way of weekly expenses and accommodation and take it from there. Within three days the deal was wrapped up and I was scheduled to leave at the end of my Leeds commitments. Whilst I earnestly hoped that it would be the middle of May, the way things were looking at the time at Headingley, I would not have been surprised to be ringing Qantas for seat availability during April!

One thing that was not affected at Leeds was the dressing-room atmosphere, a strange mixture of ritual, superstition, habit and most significantly humour, especially through the week. The majority of it centres on endless mickey-taking both before and after training and is frequently based on individual performances during either ball work exercises, sprinting or stamina. I have to take my fair share, particularly after long-distance running, and any incidents in, say, touch and pass are magnified out of all proportion back in the confines of the dressing-room. The advent of weights as an integral part of the fitness programme has given the backs the chance to exploit their prowess and a lot of them are on a par with the strength of the forwards who are frequently reminded of the fact. By the same token, if a second rower outsprints a centre, for example, they will not be allowed to forget it in a hurry. It is all meant and taken in fun at the appropriate time, but come a match day hopefully we are all totally switched on to thinking about the opposition and the prospects for our own game and how we are going to contribute to the team performance. The talking on the pitch tends to be done by the more outgoing characters, especially Colin Maskill, who often 'gees up' the forwards at the heart of the action and leads them in the defensive line. Ellery as the captain will do the main communicating but it is also down to myself and Andy Gregory to organise our attack. In the heart of the battle "sledging" has always been evident, with certain players announcing their intentions in advance, but it is far more prevalent in the Australian game and came as a shock and a surprise when I first ventured out there at club level.

It had become evident, even after only the first two matches of the season, that the new interpretation of the laws on high tackling were going to cause a problem for all the players and that Fred Lindop, as Controller of Referees, was going to have severe difficulties in maintaining that they were consistently applied. The tendency to penalise any contact above the shoulder level, irrespective of whether malice was intended, was moving the sport away from one of its traditional elements. Coupled with the law that forbids any form of ball stealing, the game is in danger of becoming touch and pass. No one involved in playing it would condone any form of premeditated violence, but historically the first ten or fifteen minutes of a match have featured a softening up period in an attempt to gain a territorial and psychological advantage. It was an integral facet of the game that the public enjoyed coming to see, a true test of strength and character. Nowadays the sides are being kept apart for too long and the pattern of play constantly interrupted by a stream of penalties. Spectators do not pay a lot of hard-earned money to see the performance of referees, they want to watch their favourites in action. The supposed increase in the number of high tackles had not seen a greater incidence of serious injuries but there was a further inconsistency in that the same offence two years before had led to instant dismissal and an almost automatic eight week ban rather than allowing culprits to stay on the pitch, as was now the case.

Hunslet (Home) - John Smith's Yorkshire Cup, Round One 13/9/92

The arrival of the County Cup game gave us a chance to divert attention away from our intensely disappointing start to the league campaign and offered us an opportunity to play host to our Third Division neighbours. Everybody rightly predicted and expected a big morale boosting victory but without any disrespect to such opponents no matter how hard you try to combat the feeling, it can be difficult to motivate yourself to play against them. Conversely they have no such problems for many regard the occasion and opportunity as one of the highlights of their career. In this tie, if anything, we started off too well, going 20-0 up inside twenty-five minutes and failing to sustain the pressure by thinking that we were going to let the crowd enjoy this and playing to them instead of the game plan. Before we knew it, we had already been pegged back to 20-10 at half-time and we had allowed Hunslet back into the match. We did not get a roasting at the interval, that is not Dougie's way, he just stressed the need to revert back to the things we had been doing well. Again, basic errors at the start of the second half continued to surrender the initiative and to their credit Hunslet gave us the fight of our lives, refusing to capitulate right to the final whistle and by the end we were lucky to escape with a shaky 28-20 victory. Defeat would have been unthinkable and an unbearable embarrassment for all connected with the club and we knew that we had still failed to earn any respect for ourselves. The seemingly continual problem of taking the wrong options was a worrying factor and criticism of our "ageing pack" was being increasingly made. Although the majority of them were over thirty, what they lacked in mobility they more than made up for in experience and, perhaps more crucially, there were few alternatives.

Whilst the first victory was always going to be important it was hardly a professional performance and the Hunslet lads quite reasonably pointed out to us that we were hardly going to set the Championship alight if they had nearly turned us over. Much was starting to be made by this time of a supposed lack of team spirit within the squad, which was not actually true as there was no conflict whatsoever. On the Tuesday night following the Hunslet match the club arranged to take all the players and their partners, directors and coaching staff out for a Chinese meal. One of the problems of having a cosmopolitan squad comprised of players from Lancashire and various nationalities is that they rarely get the chance to socialise together, especially after training if they have distances to travel. Such gestures definitely work in promoting greater harmony and developing relationships but you cannot do it just once a season for it to be really effective and beneficial. You have to organize something like that every four or five weeks to bring everybody together, especially the long-suffering other halves who have the chance to meet and develop interests and friendships with their counterparts.

The second round draw threw up an early chance to test whether my decision not to take up Hull's offer had been a wise one, although naturally I would have preferred the tie at Headingley rather than the Boulevard where I knew I would be assured of my usual unwarranted reception. Despite my having left there six years before the personal abuse from some quarters still appeared to be getting worse even though I had never given anything other than my best for the five years that I was there. I made 117 appearances alongside some tremendous players like Topliss, Skerrett, Norton, Crane and Crooks who brought the best out of me, and I managed to score 107 tries so it is disappointing still to be pilloried by a section of the fans. A factor at the back of my mind in weighing up whether to accept the player-coaching job was wondering whether they would support,

20

respect and accept me and to be honest I doubted if they would have.

Although I am now starting to achieve milestones within the game, I do not go out consciously to set records or harbour such ambitions or cravings. Neither do I take a lot of notice of personal match statistics such as tackle counts, because every game is different and as soon as it is over it is history and has no bearing on your next performance. By the same token, I do not even watch videos to analyse how I played on any particular week as I firmly believe in the theory that you are only as good as your last game.

Trying to pierce the Hunslet defence *(Credit - Peter Heston)*

22

On the burst *(Credit - Peter Heston)*

Chapter Three

False Dawn and Humiliation

In common with most types of employment there is always the likelihood that once something becomes routine there is a danger of boredom setting in. That can be the case with repetitious training routines where the motivation and desire are superseded by a sense of going through the motions. To combat that happening a crucial role for the fitness co-ordinator is to find variation in the work strategy to enable players to look forward to coming in and enjoying what they are doing. For the early weeks of the season, the drills remained fairly consistent and were based heavily on the new players getting to know what was expected of them in terms of harnessing their individual talents into the team's pattern of play. Doug's main role is on the management rather than the coaching side and when the squad split up to practise specific moves, his assistant Gary Stephens did a lot of work with the forwards whilst Andy Gregory and myself tended to look after the backs. Both sets come together for the game plan and in particular to co-ordinate defensive work on the tackle bags, which was another innovation brought over by the 1982 Aussies and tended to spoil the illusion that training should only consist of a few laps, a light-hearted and lightweight offering of touch and pass and a brisk jog to the pub. Doug and Gary came up with specific ideas and tactics to pinpoint and eliminate our own faults and to concentrate on specific areas in which our next opponents were weak or strong. Most of that analysis comes from studying match videos and statistics and takes up a good proportion of the modern coach's time as he seeks to find the best ways of exploiting his team's advantages.

It is also important to have an input from the staff about areas of your personal game that may need sharpening, honing or maintaining, but having listened to that advice I have always believed in doing my own work and concentrating on what is best for me and my body. That is especially true with regard to the treatment of injuries. I have gone on record as saying that I will not touch or play under the influence of pain-killing injections, in fact, I will not even take an aspirin for a headache, I prefer to try and let my body recover as naturally as possible. It is up to the conscience of each player as to what is acceptable for him but there is an undoubted risk that by playing on some are merely delaying the inevitable and running the risk of suffering much more severe long term damage. There are instances where coaches will ask their charges if they are prepared to play with injections if they feel that player is vital for a certain game, but as far as I am concerned if the injury is going to be better for having a week's rest then that is the best route to take.

Hull Kingston Rovers (Home) - Stones Bitter Championship 20/9/92

The Hull KR match marked my first game of the season as captain owing to Ellery's injury absence. Much has been written and debated about the issue, not least amongst the Leeds fans, and the job of skipper is very important to me. I was disappointed and upset to lose it when Ellery was signed as I have always felt that the extra responsibility was not only enjoyable but helped my game. The added involvement in the side's organisation tends to bring out the best in me, but the converse argument

26

used by some critics that when I am not captain I lose interest is not only wholly untrue but extremely infuriating.

For the first time in the season everything seemed to click for the side over the full eighty minutes. Our organisation, discipline and control showed remarkable improvement and with all due respect to the opposition we were never really tested and once we had a few points on the board we were able to generate a measure of confidence, cohesion and determination and finally start to reap the rewards of what we had practised unopposed in training. There is great pleasure gained by everyone when the attacking and defensive ploys perfected during the week are well executed in the heat of a match. Over a season that may only happen four or five times but when it does come off it is a brilliant feeling for the players and really appreciated by the spectators.

There was plenty of satisfaction to be gained from my own performance. I was directly involved in the creation of most of the tries, mainly as a result of being afforded a lot of room to make time for the players around me to exhibit their skills. I was rewarded with the club's Man of the Match award although I have learnt not to take them too seriously, especially as it does not guarantee anything come the next match. Whilst being grateful to the sponsors and selectors for their recognition, it is not something that I go out to seek, merely a bonus, and I have occasionally been awarded it when I did not deserve it or wondered what more I would have had to have done to achieve it.

More importantly, the game marked the first real opportunity of the season to acknowledge the support and loyalty of the fans in sticking by us despite our lack of success. It was also a relief to get the first league win under our belts and a welcome two points to start the season rolling, but we were determined not to get carried away and realised that we had only scratched the surface of our potential and still had a lot of hard work to do, not least with the prospect of two extremely tough away games to follow in the week ahead.

27

The training pattern obviously has to change when preparing for a mid-week match. Instead of swimming on a Monday to aid muscular recuperation from the previous day's exertions, we undertook a full training session which was repeated on the Tuesday, where normally there would have been a rest day before a game. The major problem encountered by the players prior to an evening kick-off is the boredom of waiting during the day. Most of us are family men and up around 8.00 a.m. and in spite of maybe a mid-afternoon sleep or a lie down to relax, the body and mind can easily become lethargic with the waiting around and expending of nervous energy. Having met at Headingley at the appointed time for the journey away, the priority switches to thinking about the task ahead. This is normally achieved by showing a compilation video of our good positive points from previous performances, as opposed to the video of our mistakes from the last match which is shown through the week in the lead up to a game in an effort to recognise and eliminate errors.

Hull (Away) - John Smith's Yorkshire Cup Round Two 23/9/92

Arriving at the Boulevard evoked the usual host of memories. My relationship with the current Hull officials under Chairman Stephen Watson has improved immensely since my dispute with the club and I knew that I would be guaranteed a genuinely warm reception and welcome. I certainly bear no grudges, the two directors who were responsible for dragging my name and reputation through the mud, Roy Waudby and John Rawlings, are no longer influential within the club. At the time I refused to speak to the press about the events, feeling that matters should have been left to try and resolve between us rather than in public. I was looking for a little bit more money which I felt I deserved by virtue of my achievements but the main dispute was a contract wrangle that had been

28

going on for between twelve to fourteen months beforehand.

Despite it only being the fifth match of the season, the catalogue of injuries afflicting the club was starting to mount up and become a disruptive factor, affecting the continuity of the side. We faced Hull without Alan Tait, Kevin Iro, Andy Gregory, Gary Mercer and Ellery Hanley, illustrating the need for a successful side to have a squad of twenty-two players in order to accommodate the physical demands at the top level. Key injuries are accepted as being an inevitable consequence of the challenge for honours rather than an excuse and the clamour for able, versatile deputies is a constant one. The delay to what was already a late kick-off time of 8.00 p.m.was particularly frustrating. Extensive physical warm up and psychological focusing are an integral and essential part of a side's individual and collective preparation, and a disruption of the meticulous planning that aims for achieving a peak at the kick-off can be crucial. We were informed of the fifteen minute delay to enable all the crowd to get in as we were about to run out, but discovered that this was a tactical ploy when, dispatching two of our backroom staff to the gate to assess the situation, they reported only seeing the proverbial three men and a dog waiting around outside. The onus must be on the game's administrators to make sure clubs issue the necessary warnings to arrive early and start at the designated time or face the consequences of a large fine. Once the muscles have begun tensing up again and the concentration has been broken, it is difficult to build yourself up to the same state of readiness.

When I finally led the side out I was inevitably met by the now traditional chorus of jeering and abuse from a certain minority section of the crowd. Sadly, they appear to be a knot of primarily middle-aged men and women who are hardly setting a good example to a generation of younger fans around them who possibly never even saw me perform for Hull. We again seemed to dominate the first half without putting points on the board. Our improvement in defensive discipline was matched by an increasing inability to take chances and a failure to stop making basic

29

errors. On a couple of occasions I chose not to take penalty kicks for goal in an effort to keep the pressure on but again we spilled the ball on only the second or third tackle to waste the opportunity and went in 12-4 down at the interval. The dressing-room talk, though, was naturally positive at half-time, we knew we had the match of the Hull pack and more pace in the backs and, even after going further behind early in the second period, we showed a great deal of spirit and belief to haul the match back to 18-16 as time began to run out. Perhaps the most telling blow was again self-inflicted when Dean ran on with instructions from the bench and told us that there were only six or seven minutes to go and to try and throw the ball about a little bit more in an effort to force a result. Later we found out that there were still about fifteen minutes left at that time and our attempts to play "catch-up" football rather than adopting a more disciplined approach, may have cost us the chance of victory. My try that seemed to act as the springboard for our comeback brought no greater satisfaction because it was against Hull. I had no special point to prove, it was just part of trying to do my job. The fact that we did not ultimately succeed was all that mattered to me.

A lot of debate is centred around the value of the County Cups in the current structure of the game and several knowledgeable people, including some coaches, had called them tin pot trophies. However, the fact remains that irrespective of the tradition they embody, if you win them you can justifiably call yourselves the best team in Yorkshire or Lancashire for twelve months no matter what your crowd potential or success in other spheres. It was again extremely disappointing that Leeds as the biggest club in the game would not be competing for that honour. Nevertheless, there were some encouraging signs. After the game we felt that we had lost it rather than Hull had won and that we had been on top for sixty-five out of the eighty minutes without delivering the killer blow. The following day was set aside for reporting in any niggling injuries or strains that required treatment and to recover from the inevitable bruises in the sauna and bath before picking up the training again on the Friday morning and Saturday afternoon.

That weekend marked a month before the World Cup Final and although the bandwagon was really starting to roll, I had been thinking about the game ever since the end of the tour. Even before the season started I knew that I would have to be performing well week in and week out to claim a spot. I realized that Andy Gregory, now out of retirement for this match, and Deryck Fox, would be vying for the scrum half berth leaving Shaun Edwards and myself to battle for the stand-off role. Since returning from that summer stint I had kept my eye on our likely rivals through Sky's coverage of the Australian Winfield Cup games and was under no illusions about what or who to expect.

Bradford Northern (Away) - Stones Bitter Championship 27/9/92

If you put twenty-five thousand people in Odsal Stadium it still would not have much atmosphere for the players. The stands and terraces are so far away from the pitch and the bowl so cavernous that very few sides enjoy playing there. Normally, however, Leeds and Bradford derby matches do generate an extra spice but the way we performed that day did not give our supporters anything at all to cheer about. The fact that we gave Bradford the space to play without pressurising them in the early stages allowed them to get early points on the board and generate confidence. You cannot afford to do that against any First Division side these days but against the calibre of players in the Northern team we were committing suicide and were ultimately destroyed. Their side needed little motivation anyway and was again sprinkled with the recent addition of ex-Lioners Roy Powell and David Heron to add to Paul Medley and now Deryck Fox who had been so close to joining us at Headingley and definitely had a point to prove. No

31

one had to tell us about how poorly we had played in the first half, where a lack of team work, passion and basic understanding had led to us being 22-0 down without ever really threatening a counter-attack. In the dressing-room Dougie did not really lay into us as it is not his way to shout and bawl. We knew our efforts had been nowhere near good enough and that to stand any chance of coming back into the game we would have to raise our standard by at least ninety per cent. Ellery had his say and the rest of us tried to gee each other up and for the first fifteen minutes or so of the second half we were more determined and the better side on balance. As the game went on and again panic set into our play to try and make up such a large deficit, Bradford got their second wind and proceeded to finish as they had started by ruthlessly punishing our mistakes. Perhaps our only chance would have been if the fog had drifted in more quickly and forced an abandonment. Certainly, if the match had kicked off at 3.30 as they used to do at Odsal, then it may not have finished. As I was about to kick off at the start of the second half I mentioned to referee Robin Whitfield that as he knew I wore glasses and that I could not see the far set of posts the game should have been cancelled. He advised me that it did not matter because he could not see them either and to get on with it, so our only real chance of salvaging a result was gone. The weather was never a factor, it was just an unprofessional display on the day and I was the first to own up to having had a very poor game.

I did feel that in certain sections of the media particularly that I was made a scapegoat for the team's performance, but I am only human and under Dougie at that time I had played around forty-five games and had performed badly on four occasions which was not too bad an average. The main thrust of the criticism against me, especially on the post-match phone-ins, was that if I was not captain then I was not bothered, but I have always accepted Dougie's decision to give the job to Ellery and he had held the role for over a season while I just got on with my designated role. You have to keep your own emotions and feelings private and separate from your public persona and come to terms with personal criticism in your own time and space. I am a bit of a loner, I like to think about and evaluate things on my own rather than confide in anyone else and to analyse what I did wrong and how to rectify it. To be honest, I have not come across many people whom I can trust or whose advice I would seek or respect apart from David Creasser, Lee Crooks and my youngest brother, Colin. The personal criticism did annoy and upset me and made me wonder if everything I had put into the club over the previous four or five years had been worthwhile. Some people were even prepared to regard my non-appearance on *Boots 'n All* the following evening as a failure to handle the inevitable criticism but that was not the case. The reason for my absence was purely down to the weather. The week before our flight back to Leeds on the Tuesday morning had been diverted to East Midlands Airport and I had not arrived back home until quarter to twelve after training had started at eleven. Fog was forecast again that week and, apart from being fined if I had missed the session, I knew that after such a display it was important to get back into it as quickly as possible. I have always been prepared to take the necessary flak, unlike some sports people who will milk the going while it is good and disappear if it turns sour.

The club, of course, cannot hide from its explanations and responsibilities although because of its profile and the ceaseless demands for stories about it there is often a surfeit of gossip and rumour, a lot of it either unsubstantiated or informed guesswork. On the Tuesday we had our usual full team meeting and a lot of things that mattered were thrashed out in private. We stated several home truths to each other and Dougie added that the door was open for anyone who did not want to commit themselves to Leeds Rugby League or to play for him. He reiterated that such a display was unacceptable for any First Division side and all the players could see that he really meant it and that we would have to pull our fingers out. I firmly believe that once you leave Leeds and its facilities the only way to go is downhill. Everyone had the opportunity to voice his opinion or

33

concerns but only about four or five said their piece, and as is often the case in all team sports, it is not always those who make the loudest noise in public. There was undoubtedly a grim determination to get back on the field as quickly as possible and make amends.

The shame of Odsal *(Credit - Peter Heston)*

Chapter Four

No Hiding Place

I felt that prior to the Warrington game which had been earmarked for national consumption via Sky's coverage, that it was "all eyes on Schofield, let's see how he reacts now". There seems to be a ludicrous correlation between my form and the fortunes of the side as a whole, and that if I do not play well then the team will struggle. We are not a one-man side and I cannot be expected to do everything. The Regal Trophy draw which looked like it would send us to Saints in the first round was similar to the previous year when we had to visit that week's opponents and the then defending holders, Warrington. Judging on the respective league form it looked likely to be the stiffest of tasks although not, we felt, one that was beyond us. The signing of Hunslet utility player, James Lowes, that week indicated the need to find young talent that could put pressure on the first choice players and strengthen the squad. I initially thought he had been brought as cover for me, but it looked likely that Colin Maskill was going to have to be the first to respond to the challenge.

Warrington (Home) - Stones Bitter Championship 2/10/92

The players who failed to produce the goods at Odsal were always going to be given the chance to redeem themselves in the next fixture. Perhaps the greatest single weakness of the club at the time was that there really was no one in the "A" team pushing for inclusion and challenging for a place.

Despite Andy Gregory and Gary Mercer still suffering from medium term injuries, that side on the night looked and felt like a winning outfit and we produced the kind of spirited first half needed to restore our own belief and reputations. It was particularly gratifying not so much because it was under the microscopic glare of the cameras but because it was in front of our own fans who, despite the Bradford débacle and the prospect of a warm armchair, turned out in atrocious conditions to lend their usual vociferous support. All talk of viewing this clash as a personal crusade was the furthest thing from my mind. I was not playing with additional motivation, just a renewed determination to do the job that I was paid for. That night it was to confront and overcome the then in form half back combination in the First Division of Greg Mackey and Kevin Ellis. I had no intention of altering my style to suit them, my philosophy, which my father has always told me, is to not worry about the pedigree of your opposite number, but to let him try and stop you and there was little doubt that between us Gareth Stephens and I got the better of them by doing what we did best.

Despite the incessant rain before and throughout the match we had no intention of letting the conditions dictate our play and curbing our plan to throw the ball about and to try and get it wide quickly. The fact that we managed generally to keep hold of the ball and improve our close support play and gang tackling led to calls in certain quarters for us to play all our games in a downpour. The first scores are always important but the opening try of this encounter was also a personal landmark in being my one hundredth for the club. I stated when I finally came to Leeds in October 1987 that I would like to achieve a century within five years and I managed to do it three weeks before that self-imposed deadline. One of the key elements in the victory was a change in our defensive pattern that enabled our forwards in particular to dominate the opposition. Most sides currently operate a variation on the sliding defence but that was not really working for us, and we had decided to revert back to straight man-to-man marking. With a sliding defence you can end up in situations where three men may be marking five and if you have not got outstanding pace in the side you can get caught out wide. With man-to-man marking responsibility shifts to each player and if you miss your first up tackle then you cannot blame anyone else. That decision was made by the players themselves when Dougie asked us if we were happy operating the sliding system and we told him of our preference which led to the change. The success of it in this match and the seemingly greater cohesiveness and communication was more a reflection of what we were aiming for generally, rather than a direct response to the week's criticism and speculation. What did undoubtedly help was the great buzz when walking out that night and feeling the fervour of the crowd who by rights could have been excused from lending their support in view of it being a wet Friday after one of our worst displays. Their infectious enthusiasm was felt on the pitch and provided further inspiration and encouragement to repay their faith in us. Their appreciation over the entire eighty minutes was invaluable and we responded with some good football, tight defence and an effective kicking game.

Apart from the obvious importance of gaining two vital league points we needed that kind of disciplined performance to generate confidence for the forthcoming encounter at Wigan. The weekend off gave us a little extra time to recover from any knocks prior to the unenviable task of going to Central Park.

Wigan (Away) - Stones Bitter Championship
11/10/92

Rather than perhaps being a "Test trial" for a lot of the players involved in the game prior to selection of the Great Britain squad for the World Cup Final, the match at Wigan was more of an assessment of how far Leeds had come since their end of the season humiliation there in the Premiership semi-final the previous May. Our highest ever defeat, 74-6, had left a bitter taste throughout the club and offered a chance to chart our progress against the best. Our build up through the week followed its normal pattern without placing any special emphasis on the significance of the opposition. Although there is still a variance in standard between the teams in the First Division you can no longer afford to take any of them lightly or treat any of them differently. Every game is very hard and requires maximum concentration and we certainly were not going to Wigan with a defeatist attitude or expecting to cave in. The return of the contingent of ex-Wiganers in the side, Shaun Wane, Andy Goodway and Ellery Hanley with Andy Gregory and Kevin Iro on the sidelines, was less of an issue than people might have expected. All of them are the ultimate professionals and were more concerned with doing their best for Leeds rather than trying to show the Wigan board and public that they had made a mistake in letting them go. Central Park is an extremely imposing venue and perhaps the only one that approaches Headingley. It can be a daunting place even to do a warm-up against a background of noise which, by the time the home side are about to emerge from the tunnel, has risen to a deafening roar. As with most encounters against the top sides, the increased speed and intensity of the game is quickly evident and a major facet of the way Wigan play. Naturally, it was a very tough encounter although again the vital softening-up period was disrupted by the new interpretation of the head tackle law that served only to break up the play and prevented the forwards from attempting some of the bigger hits that make their mark on the match and which the crowd still want to see. We stuck at it in spite of again conceding points from our own mistakes, particularly missing first-up tackles, which Wigan ruthlessly punished. Their forwards were consistently making the advantage line and coming in waves which is their trademark, and their half-backs of Shaun Edwards and Frano Botica were feeding their three-quarters who were getting on the outside of us.

Even being 16-0 down at the interval we were not ashamed of our display and showed a lot of composure and spirit in the second half when we took the game to them. At half-time we knew that despite the score in the opening period Wigan had not been that much better than us. Far from viewing the remainder of the game as an exercise in damage limitation and keeping the score line down we were convinced that we could create enough chances to score at least sixteen points ourselves. In the end we lost the second half 8-6 and were beaten by the better side but we took some encouragement from certain aspects of our effort and the game was not as one-sided as the newspaper headlines and final score line suggested. Having played the two top sides in the opening weeks, Saints and Wigan, we knew the standard we had to aspire to and that to overcome them we would need to improve our close support play as every time they had made even a half break they always had five or six players backing up. Wigan continue to be the benchmark by which we assess our progress on all aspects of defensive organisation and attacking efficiency.

For Leeds, the first quarter of the season had been a very disappointing start but there was an underlying feeling about the club that when all the talent was available we would still be able to make an impact. We knew that our full strength side was going to be a force and that had been recognised by some of the more discerning pundits in the game. We had not really given ourselves a settling in time but in a reverse of our fortunes in the previous season, we expected to be running into our best form

Attempting to beat the covering Billy McGinty *(Credit - Martin Robson)*

around Christmas when the serious issues in the league began to be sorted out and in time for a real run at the Challenge Cup. Attention now shifted to the World Cup Final as speculation mounted as to the likely composition of the squad and the captaincy. I would have been disappointed if I had not got the job as I felt that I had not let anyone down in that capacity on the tour. Whilst I had no intention of changing my preparation from that for any normal game I already knew a fortnight beforehand that I would be more apprehensive and possibly even nervous about this occasion than for any other match. Its significance for the sport as a whole could not be underestimated and the excitement of a central involvement beckoned. I have always believed that having gained a good living out of the game it is essential to return something and in that way I have always been conscious of trying to be a good ambassador for the sport. When I was a youngster and players like Kevin Dick and Peter Muscroft were doing presentations to me as a schoolboy it left a tremendous impression and fired my ambition to try and become a professional player and emulate that sort of standard. Having now reached that fortunate position, if I have time I like to remain involved in spreading the virtues of the game at all levels. I never really had boyhood idols or heroes but the two people who had the major influences on my career as a kid were my father, Geoff and my Hunslet Parkside Coach, Ron Tinker. The two players who brought me along at a time when I was just starting to develop were David Topliss, who was a fantastic help to play outside of and made sure that I could not fail in the successful Hull side of the mid-eighties, and Peter Sterling, who was the greatest player I have every played with. In spite of being only five foot five inches tall his game had everything and he was an absolute genius.

Chapter Five

Cometh the Hour

About a week before the official announcement Malcolm Reilly informed me of his intention to retain me as the Great Britain Captain, a decision that made me both happy and relieved. I was under no illusions that with Ellery likely to be recalled to the squad and with him having led the international side in his last nineteen or twenty Tests, he might have been reinstated in the role. Malcolm's call was very reassuring and morale boosting and the thought of leading the team out in the most important single game for over twenty years and at the national stadium with a wave of fervent support behind us was quite incredible. I have always been intensely patriotic and the obvious pride associated with such a tremendous honour was balanced by a measure of apprehension about the build-up and importance of the match for the code as a whole, as it for once took centre stage in the sporting calendar. The media interest from all sectors and most especially and unusually the national press and television was a daunting prospect no matter how enjoyable. For everyone involved with or interested in British Rugby League this was a unique opportunity to get the game discussed and hopefully remembered throughout the land and with the right result an impact akin to the 1966 Soccer World Cup.

The official announcement of the captaincy marked the pinnacle of my career in the game to date. In professional sport there is always the opportunity for material rewards as you progress through the game but once you have spent it or retired there may be very little to show for the efforts. Memories, however, can never be taken away from you and last for as long as you live. Some journalists had tried to make an issue out of the politics of the captaincy in an effort to generate a story like the ones constantly floating around Leeds, but Ellery came up to me as soon as he found out, we shook hands and he genuinely congratulated me.

The weekend prior to the final was fortunately a blank one for Leeds with Wakefield's involvement in the Yorkshire Cup Final and I could concentrate fully on the forthcoming event. For the bulk of the British squad though, it was business as usual which was a particular worry for the team management who were unable to finalise the last week's build-up and preparations before knowing the fitness and availability of the players. There was the added ludicrous situation of Wigan meeting St. Helens in the Lancashire Cup Final only six days prior to the Wembley confrontation in a full-blooded, intense local derby in which just over half the Great Britain squad were involved. The anxious wait until Monday to assess the injury situation undoubtedly disrupted some of the advanced planning. Fortunately all the players came through and no major changes were required. With a limited time to work together the training emphasis switched primarily to perfecting set moves and a full understanding of the game plan rather than concentrating on fitness. This was especially critical with regard to the defensive ploys as each club worked to a varying system and co-ordination in the line is a vital aspect. Throughout the training we worked on playing to a very tight pattern within our own twenty-five and then opening the ball out as soon as the position allowed it. The plan had been well established under Malcolm and his assistant Phil Larder, and even though Phil had now taken up the managerial reins himself at Widnes and relinquished the Great Britain role, we were well versed in its demands and execution. His replacement, John Kear, had worked alongside Phil in the National Coaching Scheme for over a year and had been on the summer tour and was easily able to pick up where Phil had left off and continue his methods.

I had already watched the Aussies in their warm-up match at Sheffield although we knew what the composition and capability of their Test side would be and its consequent strengths and weaknesses. Their expected victories over Huddersfield, Sheffield and Cumbria did not cause us any great concern or any need to revise our thinking. The atmosphere between the two camps embodied the true essence of the sport, our increasing familiarity and the closeness of the summer series had led to the building of a mutual respect and this was reflected off the field, particularly with regard to the promotional events for the match. I travelled down to London by train with Graham Steadman, Mal Meninga and Allan Langer to attend a photo call at London Zoo and there was a genuine camaraderie between the players even at this level. Needless to say, once out on the park all that is forgotten for eighty minutes in the quest for dominance but afterwards friendships re-emerge in the bar as discussions centre on what happened during the game and on looking forward to the next challenge.

The prospect of playing at Wembley was awe-inspiring in itself. It is difficult to put into words the feeling of what the place is like and the magic it holds. You have got to go out there and smell the atmosphere really to experience it. Each time I had been, with Hull in 1985 and Great Britain in 1990, I had experienced the same terrific surge of adrenalin and feeling of disbelief when walking out into the cauldron of the arena filled to its capacity. The thrill and physical sensation of goose pimples down your entire body is impossible to describe accurately and is why the venue means so much to those privileged enough to play there, irrespective of the sport they are involved in. Far from being intimidating the place is inspiring and hopefully you go out there to enjoy yourself. The increasing demand for newspaper features and various interviews took up a fair amount of time but I realised early on that being captain and hopefully a nationally representative figure you have got to make yourself available.

I did a long piece for *Grandstand* when the cameras came to the house and profiled myself and the family. It was good for the two kids to get some recognition and they certainly loved seeing themselves on television and kept getting the tape of it out to remind themselves. Playing the match in the capital gave Rugby League the kind of exposure in the southern media which is essential if it is to expand and be taken seriously and showed the journalists that there is another game outside Rugby Union. Such efforts have not been so successful in the past. I have featured in a previous article where my photo had been captioned under the name Henderson Gill! - even the photographers who came to London Zoo expected they were on a football assignment and were busily looking around for Queens Park Rangers players. Such a lack of recognition is disappointing for the British players and bewildering for the Aussies, who are the constant centre of attention and hype back in Queensland and New South Wales. Every chance we got we stressed the importance of the match and its relevance to the sport and some of the features in the national press were considered and rewarding.

On the Monday before the game the players gathered to begin their build-up to the match which followed a fairly strict regime. We met at Headingley for fitness tests and to get the official photo calls and interviews with the press out of the way. We trained at Wigan on the Tuesday with a little fitness work and a full discussion and practice of the game plan and strategies. Particular emphasis was placed on the kicking game as a vital element in modern Test match rugby, in an effort to create the right field position to launch concerted effective attacks. On Wednesday we again met in Leeds and concentrated primarily on ball work and defensive patterns. The team was officially announced and we went into camp overnight at a hotel in Bramhope, near Leeds. Fortunately, as the nucleus of the squad had been together for a while, overcoming club loyalties and rivalries which can often be the case in some national teams was not a problem and a family atmosphere already existed. A lot of people assume that in trying to accommodate the different top personalities there will inevitably be cliques that the captain has to keep together. In the Great Britain squad we all knew our individual and combined roles and that one hundred per cent team commitment would be needed to achieve the right sort of performance against such illustrious opposition. Part of the captain's man management function is to get everyone thinking along the same lines and one of the skills is to act as the representative spokesman for the team as a whole. As in any group of people there are always some who are shy and do not know how to put their point of view across. If any of them had a problem or a worry about what they were being asked to do and did not want to approach manager Maurice Lindsay or Malcolm directly then that is hopefully where the captain steps in and generates confidence and spirit. That is perhaps the converse side to all the high profile interviews, but is no less important or enjoyable and where you need to earn the ultimate respect from your fellow professionals. I have been fortunate enough to play under a lot of good captains and gained experience from performing with them and am now at the time in my career where I can start passing some of it on. In my developing years at Hull David Topliss was a great influence in that aspect of captaincy.

As the match got nearer its implication became even more important to the players in whose hands and feet the immediate history and future of the game would be determined. I stressed to the media that if we did win we deserved to rank alongside Bobby Moore and Geoff Hurst and to the players that they could ensure themselves sporting "immortality" if they fulfilled their potential. I was not involved in consultations as to the final composition of the side but Malcolm did put it to me that he would like to use me at centre in the absences of Paul Loughlin and Darryl Powell and I readily agreed for this one-off encounter, especially having played most of my international career in that position. It seemed the ideal option and was a team selection purely to do a specific job. Part of the plan was to move to stand-off in the second half in order to play a more expansive pattern later on when the gaps would hopefully be available. Operating at centre meant a direct confrontation with Mal Meninga whom I had first encountered as an eighteen year old kid and who, along with his partner, Gene Miles, had given me a very rough baptism in top level rugby. Being older, wiser and a lot more experienced it was a challenge I was relishing and one tailor-made for the media coverage who sought to personalise the duel rather than look at team contributions which is a player's primary concern. I did not anticipate that moving away from the heart of play would make the captain's job any harder, it is just as easy to be heard at centre and I certainly like to talk a lot on the pitch, some have said too much! It is not a matter of shouting or ranting but more of offering encouragement and enthusiasm, patting players on the back, trying to boost their morale and hopefully leading by example to get the best out of them.

Wakefield (Away) - Stones Bitter Championship 21/10/92

Whilst in camp at the hotel the Leeds contingent heard that the side had again gone down away from home, this time in the last minute of the rearranged league fixture at Belle View. Our reaction was that even without the three current internationals but with Andy Gregory returning from his six week lay-off the team should have been strong enough to win, especially when we learnt that they had surrendered a half-time 16-4 lead. Having gained such a commanding position, even though down to twelve men, they should have been able to close the game down and wait for Wakefield to make mistakes playing "catch up" football. On this occasion, not for the first time in the season, it seemed to work in reverse and we appeared to lose the plot and let them back into the game. Although we had not seen the match there was a sense of disbelief about the result and the circumstances of the loss, the winning point having been scored with the last kick.

The Great Britain squad trained at Headingley at 10.00 a.m. the following morning before departing for our Hertfordshire headquarters around midday. By then it had been officially announced that Graham Steadman would be unfit to take his place in the side but that did not disrupt our preparations as we had known from the outset that the way he had been training he would not be in realistic contention. He had been able to take part at less than half pace and was continually limping so we had planned for Joe Lydon to be playing at full back and the late decision was timed, more to confuse the Aussies than anything else. We arrived at the hotel around 3.45 p.m. by which time stories were filtering out, mainly attributed to Shaun Edwards, that we were unhappy about the choice of Kiwi Dennis Hale as referee. In view of his performance in the summer Ashes series it was a genuine concern, for we felt that not only had some of his interpretations of the rules been open to question but that he had actually been influenced by the Australian management. No sooner had we arrived than we were back on the bus at 4.30 p.m. in our suits to attend an official reception at the Queen Elizabeth Conference Centre with the Heritage Minister Peter Brooke, various MPs and High Commissioners, the Rugby League hierarchies of the two respective countries and a few of the Australian squad players who were not involved in the match. The cameras followed us there as we completed our promotional duties, after which we retired to an Italian restaurant to stock up our pasta intake. From that point on as a squad we tried to cut ourselves off from the inevitable hype and focus on the job in hand which the media seemed to understand. By the time we got back to the hotel, which was an hour's drive from London, it was around 10.30 p.m. and the end of a long, tiring 12 hour day which was hardly ideal planning but supposedly necessary. We voiced an opinion that only a few representatives of the side and the captain should have attended, like the Australians, but that was deemed to be inappropriate.

On the Friday morning prior to the match most of the squad visited Wembley with the exception of the Wigan contingent who were becoming used to its unique surroundings after so many recent visits there in the Challenge Cup Final. They preferred to stay at the hotel and study the day's horse racing form. Malcolm and I gave our last interviews for BBC TV *Sport on Friday* whilst at the stadium, before the final stage of the preparation began. A certain amount of it centred around watching and analysing motivational videos, most of which comprised of action culled from the summer tour. Some highlighted the negative points to work on where we had conceded tries and others illustrated positive aspects of our play where we had taken the Aussies on and beaten them. I am a firm believer in not dwelling too long on history and that there is a limited value in reminiscing on past achievements. The top players know their capabilities and the areas of their game which they have to work on and, besides, if anyone was having difficulty getting motivated for this encounter, then they should not have been playing.

Official World Cup photocall at Headingley (*Credit - Graham Clay*)

Chapter Six

The World Cup Final

I slept well the night before possibly the most significant match of my career. I had stressed to the players the need for concentration and enthusiasm throughout the training but equally important for them to cope with the mounting pressure was to find time to relax and to avoid thinking about the match constantly. Focusing and visualising your role in advance is an essential part of preparation but unless you can maintain a level headed approach then nervous energy is just wasteful and apprehension gets in the way of proper eating and rest. The players were encouraged to do their own thing the night before, some played cards or snooker, others watched television or stayed in their rooms with a cup of tea. On the morning of the game that low key approach was maintained. We met at 10.00 a.m. for our pre-match meal consisting of baked beans on toast or pasta or rice pudding and fruits and the majority of the players were calm, smiling and in the right frame of mind. After that we went for a twenty minute walk during which Malcolm went round each individual reminding them of their specific tasks before the players changed into their suits and we had our own team meeting where I had a few quiet words with the lads and so did Ellery.

By the time we got on the bus at 12.15 for the forty minute drive to Wembley, we were completely switched on to the task in hand. In order to keep themselves calm a lot of the squad preferred listening to music on walkmans, as this worked for them on a week-to-week basis at club level. There was no attempt to alter their preferred routines and they would not have responded to an imposed regime anyway. The nerves tended to start as we got nearer to Wembley and began to get caught up in the colourful sway of people heading towards the ground and their cheering and chanting as they saw us approaching. It was a tremendous sight, travelling down Wembley Way amongst the multitude of club jerseys all mingling with each other and justifying the tremendous interest in the encounter. The way they got behind us as we stepped off the coach gave us a tremendous feeling and a terrific boost. We assembled in the dressing-room and Maurice Lindsay and I agreed that the squad should go out on to the pitch together and stay out there for ten minutes in order to acknowledge the fans and to soak up the atmosphere. Back in the changing area the players started their own rituals for getting ready, some are very superstitious or follow fastidious practices for strapping or stretching whilst others continually listen to specific music. The size of the Wembley dressing-rooms, like those at Headingley, allows for individual preparation. I was keeping an eye on everyone, checking they were all right, cajoling them and helping them to keep relaxed and not tense up. Adopting that role for everyone else eases your own state of mind but it is at times like that where personal strength of character and self discipline and belief are particularly important. Even though I was a little bit nervous I had to hide it from the others and set the lead, although that suited me as I do not like showing my emotions. About fifteen minutes prior to walking out Malcolm called everyone together and briefly outlined the team objectives for the last time, after which I gave a few words of encouragement before lining up to lead the side out.

Walking up the tunnel brought home the meaning and value of the captaincy. There is nothing to compare with walking out into the wall of sound, noise, colour and this time smoke from the cannons that is a unique part of a Wembley occasion. It was almost unbelievable and a moment that I will never forget or tire of recalling. It would have been easy to get carried away in such surroundings but it was a deliberate policy when walking out only to look forward and appear purposeful. This is something that has emanated from the Wigan influence. In previous years teams have emerged waving and looking for their families and friends in the stand whereas the ideal is to remain highly concentrated on the reason why you are there and impervious to all the outside influences. Meeting the dignitaries is something that has to be done no matter how much the players want to get out there and into the action and as I went down the line I reminded them that it would soon be over and not to lose their intensity or confidence. After the emotion of the anthems and the individual player introductions I called the boys together into a circle to wish them all the best, to remind them to enjoy the occasion as much as possible and to play to the best of their ability. As long as the players give one hundred per cent and the coach knows it then there is no more anyone can ask of them. Once I was up there shaking hands and tossing the coin all the preliminaries were over and almost instantaneously it seemed the battle was underway.

The ruggedness of the early exchanges were just what we had expected and relished and led to an early penalty from Deryck Fox which was just the start and springboard that we were looking for. It was vital to seize the initiative and to try and test the débutant Aussie full back, Tim Brasher, with a bomb as quickly as possible. The ploy worked to perfection and achieved our first goal of putting the Aussies under pressure as early as possible, as they were not used to coming from behind. Even though we could not break them down we established good field position. The pin-point kicks to the corner from Deryck and the chase were excellent and the touch-finding was good when required. The first half confrontations embodied the true essence of Test match football; the referee's interpretations of the revised head tackle law, offside and scrum feeding were as he saw it, with an accent on keeping the game flowing and, to be fair, I think that overall he did pretty well in the circumstances. The crucial incident in that first half was the injury to Gary Connolly when he turned his ankle and suffered ligament damage, firstly because it prevented us from carrying out the plan of switching me to stand-off as we had to bring John Devereux on as his replacement, and secondly, because it gave Steve Renouf some latitude that until then he had not really had. That was a massive blow which was only slightly tempered by going in with a 6-4 interval lead which was something of a bonus. At half-time Malcolm stressed that the game plan was going well, that the defence was solid and that the forwards were making the initial hard yardage against a bigger and stronger pack and that we were gradually building the platform from which to spread the ball about. We knew that we had to get the ball wider second and third man out and to try to get the second rowers moving and attacking their middle and outside backs to create the space for our wingers to show their undoubted paces.

The second half opened at an even greater tempo, if that were possible, and it was a credit to the fitness levels of all the players that the intensity never dropped over the entire eighty minutes. The pace of the sides was virtually equal and the only difference turned out to be just one fatal mistake that handed them the game-breaking try. Initially, Alan Hunte dropped the ball on the first tackle on our own 25 yard line when running out from defence and then John Devereux got sucked in and allowed Steve Renouf on the outside for his début score. Prior to that we had weathered the storm of being reduced to twelve men following Shaun Edwards' sin binning for a reckless challenge for which he was lucky not to have been sent off. That incident had not disrupted us, we had rallied round each other, maintained our composure and discipline and had been looking to kick on when Shaun returned. The additional defensive duties and vigilance took a lot out of us but we had taken great confidence from not conceding any points in his absence. To then yield a try was a sickening blow but with plenty of time left it was by no means a lost cause in spite of Mal

Meninga's prodigious touch-line conversion. Talking to the lads behind the posts, I stressed that there was no need to give up hope and that all we needed to do was to prize out one clean break. As we restarted it began raining and in spite of the obvious problems with handling a wet football, that actually seemed to give us the extra confidence and impetus which we needed to camp in or around the Aussie last quarter of the pitch for ten out of the remaining thirteen minutes. As the pressure increased in those final stages so did the tendency to panic and a few times players sacrificed the game plan by trying individual breaks that were destined to fail. I took a drive in when I should not have, Martin Dermott tried a chip over the top that went dead, Deryck Fox tended to get caught in possession and Shaun found difficulties in getting the ball away from the ruck area. We came exceptionally close when Alan Tait seemed to have gathered Deryck's huge up-and-under beneath the posts, but to his credit Tim Brasher positioned himself well and stood his ground to prevent Alan grounding the ball.

We were constantly aware of the time implication but when the final hooter sounded I was engulfed by a feeling of disbelief and a sensation that the game had sped by seemingly in a matter of minutes. The total disappointment and dejection for the players and management was almost impossible to bear and was heightened by the anguish of failing to reward the seventy thousand fanatical supporters who had got behind us totally in the stadium and the millions more watching on TV worldwide, some possibly for the first time. First reflections are always steeped in the emotion of the moment but I genuinely felt that we had given it our best shot, been far from disgraced and in the end had lost to a team that had handled itself better at the height of the pressure. The BBC collared me at the side of the pitch for an instantaneous interview and reaction and although it was impossible to hide the agony and I found answering the questions difficult it is all part of the job and you know that you are going to have to do it some time and cannot run away from the responsibilities.

If we had won I would have spoken to every single person in the crowd and I am sure the side would not have left the pitch until after midnight, but if you have lost there is no hiding place and there are obligations such as collecting medals to fulfil, no matter how hard it was to drag myself up those long steps to the Royal Box. I knew that we had prepared as well as we could have, that we had worked hard in training and contributed to an enthralling, close confrontation but just failed to get the right result. The whole event had been unforgettable and we knew that we had pushed the Aussies all the way which would have been unthinkable five or six years before. All in all, no matter how much it hurt to lose, I felt that overall we had done ourselves justice, we had come so near in our quest and now had the frustration of having to wait for another two years before confronting them here again and trying to gain revenge.

Back in the dressing-room I thanked the team for their efforts and told them that no matter how deflated they were feeling that it was not the be-all and end-all of life and that they could all hold their heads up. It was pretty hard to get a response even from some of the more ebullient characters, no one really needed telling how they had played nor that they had lost the chance of a hefty bonus. The money was secondary on this occasion but it was galling to be only thirteen minutes away from one of the game's top rewards.

The slant of the majority of the questions and opinions from people after the game was that we had played the wrong tactics by not moving the ball out wide at every opportunity and bringing Martin Offiah into the play more. Such criticisms that we had been deliberately over-cautious and sacrificed our traditional expansive flair were unjustified. The simple fact was that unfortunately Australia's defence was very strong and ruthless and under those conditions there was no point in passing the ball purely for its own sake. It was a very tight game between evenly matched sides and to try and give Martin the ball when he was well away from me or covered by two or three defenders was not an option. He is an exceptional player but not a miracle worker and his opposite number Willie Carne policed him extremely well. Inside him, Mal and I tended to cancel each other out on that side of the field in what was almost a game of physical chess. If the contest had allowed us to play the so-called "British" way of throwing the ball about, like we had planned in practice, we most certainly would have, but if we had resorted to those tactics without building a solid base we would have been beaten by a far greater margin. The Aussies would have put so much more pressure on us that we would have coughed the ball up playing desperation football in the wrong part of the field and conceded demoralising tries, the result of which would have set the whole code in this country back on its heels.

I honestly felt that the game had demonstrated that the two sides had achieved a level of parity and that the only difference between them was their respective strength in depth. The first choice teams were on paper, man for man, almost equal but the structure and intensity of the Australian game breeds a reservoir of talent that we currently cannot match. Alterations to our domestic season that give the top players fewer games but at the highest standards of pressure football week in and week out are essential. It is no longer enough for players to be able to raise their game for a one-off confrontation if we are to achieve international dominance again within the sport. The World Cup Final, and its ultimate disappointment, had to be viewed as the immediate springboard for pre-planning the next Ashes series. Even though the game marked a dream come true for me I made a personal vow to try to remain centrally involved in that task, hopefully as captain until the centenary celebrations in 1995. Such an auspicious event fires the ambition, but knowing Malcolm as I do, sentiment and reputation will count for nothing in the future and only players showing consistent form at the time will warrant inclusion in his squads. In some ways the final also marked the end of an era for a generation of players such as Kevin Ward and Andy Gregory and the start of the ongoing challenge to rebuild and blood some new young talent to replace them. Without any disrespect to Shaun Edwards or Deryck Fox who have both been tremendous servants in international football, I believe that our next long term scrum half should be Bobby Goulding. Everybody knows that he has got a fiery temperament both on and off the field, but if he was brought on with that kind of long term incentive before him, I am sure it would be the spur to settle him down.

It is impossible to say, even with hindsight, if the result would have been altered in any way if I had been able to move into the stand-off role at some stage during the second half. I am sure I would have been even more closely marked than I was in the centre although I may have got the ball slightly wider at the crucial time. The other major incident that was commented on throughout the media afterwards, perhaps to the detriment of the showpiece, was Martin Offiah's walk off ahead of the rest of the side leaving the pitch. I think the significance of the whole episode may well have been exaggerated out of proportion although at the time none of us realised what had happened. Martin explained his reasoning that you do not do a lap of honour when you lose, but I did not like what he did and if I had noticed, as captain I would have called him back on. For everyone else in the squad it was a lap of appreciation in tribute to all the supporters who had followed us from the North and who are the backbone of the game and pay our wages on a weekly basis. In a way we were saying sorry to them for not getting the right result but that we had given the best we could and that hopefully we had not let them down. After the match, despite the dejection, there was an official reception attended by the entire British party at which the Australians were early arrivals. Having known them for a number of years, it is safe to say that if the boot had been on the other foot they would have been conspicuous by their absence. That had been the case after our Third Test victory in 1988 when Whitbread sponsored the post match dinner at the Sydney Hilton and only three Kangaroo players managed to find their way there. As the game was consigned to history, we all had a good night in a great spirit of camaraderie although it is fair to say

60

that the beer and wine tasted a little bit flat.

The morning after, back at the hotel, I read all the papers and the opinions of the various journalists as to what we should have done and where we went wrong even though we hardly needed telling. We left there at around 11.00 a.m. in two coaches, one bound for Yorkshire and the other for the Lancashire contingent, stopping at Watford Gap to pick up our wives and girl-friends who had also been staying in London. On returning to Leeds that Sunday evening I took the kids out for tea, not having seen them for a few days and my son, who was only two and a half, met me with 'I saw you on telly, Dad, did you win?' which only served to bring home the disappointment. On the Monday I was back down in London for *Boots 'n All* although to be honest I do not remember a lot about it except that I did not really want to sit through more post match analysis.

A picture of utter dejection *(Credit - Martin Robson)*

Chapter Seven

Back to Reality

It took me a full seven days for the result and implications of the World Cup Final really to sink in and for me to be able to think about reviewing the match on video. I still experience a tremendous sense of pride and achievement seeing the pictures of me leading the side out although right now it all seems a little unbelievable. A lot of people asked me how I would be able to come to terms with the defeat and pick up the domestic season following all the hype surrounding Wembley but as a professional player you have to learn how to put all these things behind you and concentrate on performing in the role for which you are paid by your club side. Nevertheless, it was very, very hard. That same week I watched the Brisbane Broncos put Wigan to the sword in the World Club Challenge proving again that at present, at the highest levels, we find it difficult to compete with the Aussies. Wigan have swept all before them in recent years but the margin of the Broncos' victory at Central Park, when they had not played competitively for six weeks following their own Grand Final victory, proved that the intensity and consistency generated by their schedule is superior to our own. There is no substitute for playing against the best opposition in a pressurised environment on a regular basis in order to improve your game and hone your skills. Currently, fifteen out of the sixteen Winfield Cup sides could mount a serious challenge for their

Minor Premiership but it is difficult to imagine any British side achieving the same success over there because we are just not used to those sorts of demands.

The league encounter with Widnes marked the long awaited Leeds début of Kevin Iro which not only gave the squad a big lift in training but also enabled the club to turn out a full strength side for the first time in the season. That was a timely boost for Dougie in view of the friendly rivalry that still exists with his old club and was also the first real opportunity for us to show what we were capable of and that we could still be a force to be reckoned with. Kevin's registration saw the departure from the club of his Kiwi colleague, Morvin Edwards, in order for us to satisfy our quota allowance of three overseas players. Personally, I think three imports are too many and harm the development of talent in our own game and that engaging the services of only two top class players would be sufficient.

Widnes (Home) - Stones Bitter Championship 1/11/92

In fairness to our poor start to the season, we had consistently stated that things would be different when we had all our best players on the park together and there would have been no excuses if we had not put on a convincing display against the Chemics. The game was given added interest by the return of Bobby Goulding to Headingley where he had a point to prove and, for me, the chance to play opposite Tony Myler, a player who I honestly believe on his day when he is fully fit is still our best stand-off. I have always enjoyed the challenge of pitting my skills against his and occasionally in the past he has got the better of me. We played together at Balmain in 1986 and became firm friends both on and off the field.

Games against Widnes are traditionally a physical encounter and this one proved to be no exception. Despite the ferocity of their opening exchanges, many of which were illegal, we showed great credit by not retaliating and finally displayed that our forwards could mix it with the best on defence and combined that with some impressive attacking play, even from inside our own twenty-five, now that we had the necessary pace out wide. If the referee had stamped his authority on the proceedings early on I am sure that some of the later, more malicious, cheap shots could have been avoided. The Leeds forwards and particularly the front row set the lead and started in determined fashion, for the first time dominating a pack that had come to intimidate them. From that rolling platform Andy Gregory and I had the space we needed to bring the best out of the backs. Kevin's two first half tries and storming runs were an inspiration and seemed to bring the best out of Jim Fallon who appeared to come of age playing outside him and benefited from his experience and promptings. It was unfortunate that Kevin had to retire at the interval as we were starting to play the type of attractive and enjoyable game that we aimed for in training by getting the ball wide as early as possible and showed more of a killer instinct in putting points on the board when the chances came along. Our half-time ovation was fully deserved after a devastating first forty minutes, but in the dressing-room it was necessary to calm ourselves down and realise that the job was only half done and that with the calibre of Widnes' players they were quite capable of scoring as many points as we had. On the resumption, however, they seemed more intent on keeping the score down by resorting to disruptive spoiling tactics which allowed me to kick eight goals during the match, which I could not remember having done for a very long time and was the best response to the rising tide of ill feeling. We replied with controlled aggression and discipline which prevented a full scale brawl in the face of continued provocation and inconsistency with regard to the incidence of head high tackling. Some of the Widnes players had two or three attempts before they were penalised or warned, culminating in their two sendings off, although Steve McCurrie became the victim of what had previously gone unpunished.

In the end, we finished the job in style and any controversy was immediately forgotten in the after-match bar. The Man of the Match award was pleasing recognition for my contribution but more important was the team's response to the doubters and critics and the rave reviews made a few detractors sit up and take notice of our potential. However, there was no danger of overconfidence and, as Ellery and I left the pitch, I mentioned to him that by conceding a couple of silly penalties when we really had the pressure on we had let Widnes off the hook and that point was stressed in our regular team meeting the following Tuesday. The manner of the win confirmed what we already knew rather than restoring confidence or changing our attitude. It was always going to be just a matter of time before we clicked against a good side although we were not under any illusions about the size of the task ahead or that one victory had guaranteed anything. On the same weekend our Academy side had their first exposure on Sky Sports, scoring a good away win at St. Helens in an entertaining high-scoring clash. That forward-thinking move was a great idea offering the best sixteen or seventeen year old talent an early chance to make a name for themselves and start to be noticed.

The plaudits gained after the Widnes encounter took the spotlight and scrutiny off the club and allowed us to prepare for the imposing trip to Knowlsley Road and a revenge meeting with Saints, this time in the first round of the lucrative Regal Trophy. The season before we had hit peak form to reach the final and despite being seen as the underdogs in this tie we were keen to repeat that run and hopefully go one better. I had learnt from my experiences at Leeds over the previous six years that it was easy to get carried away making predictions and rash promises about trophies being just around the corner. This time, the low key, low profile, business-as-usual build up to this next challenge for honours was exactly what was required. The spur for the whole club was the ongoing determination to

Escaping the clutches of Tony Myler for a change *(Credit - Martin Robson)*

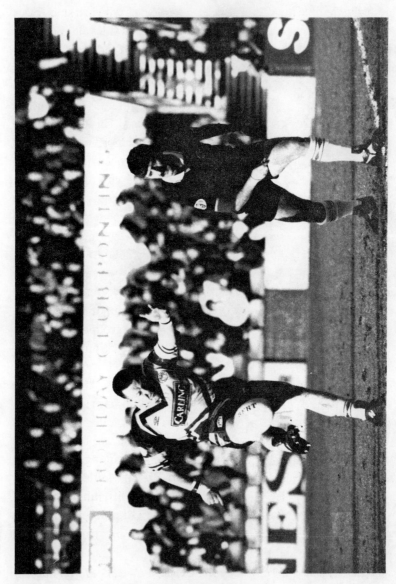

The consequences of another Widnes infringement as Ian Ollerton looks on *(Credit - Martin Robson)*

reward the incredible loyalty and patience of the fans who had stuck by us in such large numbers. Saints had been one of the form sides although their humbling home defeat by Bradford the previous weekend had done us no favours and would ensure that any complacency would have been knocked out of them and fired them up to restore their reputations in front of their own fans. We were relishing the prospect but again suffered the misfortune of a late injury withdrawal that upset our preparations. This time I was the victim during our final run through on the Saturday morning prior to the game. It was especially ironic in that the session had been held over from the day before because I had arranged to have the day off to take my daughter into hospital for an operation on her adenoids and to have grommets put in to cure a slight deafness. What made it even more frustrating was that the training itself was the best and most enjoyable session I had been involved with at Headingley for about twelve months. Everything seemed to be coming off and all the players were enthusiastic even though we were only out there for about twenty-five minutes. Around five minutes before the end, Andy Gregory threw one of his very hard passes that cut out about five men and went near to the ground and as I bent to collect it I pulled a hamstring. It was a complete accident, an occupational hazard, but I knew right away that it was pretty serious. Fortunately it was not a severe pull whereby your leg blackens but more of a knot where the blood circulation had cramped up. Up to that point I had never pulled a muscle throughout my career despite suffering a multitude of sprains and bruises but it seems that hamstring and groin injuries are becoming the curse of the modern rugby player. The cause may be training or stretching related but the main fear is one of recurrence as once the initial damage has been done the effects, like ligament strains, can be difficult to shake off entirely. I am not a very good spectator at the best of times, I do not find myself shouting advice or criticism, I just hold the frustration and annoyance inside me and silently will the boys on.

Saint Helens (Away) - Regal Trophy Round One 8/11/92

I travelled with the side on the team bus as we followed our usual ritual of picking up the Lancashire based players at a hotel in Haydock but on arriving at the ground my direct contribution ended. There is little point in cluttering up the dressing-room when space is at a premium and specific preparations are underway. It must be a nightmare for a coach to struggle to get his best team on the park, record a satisfying result when that is finally achieved and then have the pattern and continuity upset by a late withdrawal the next week. Craig Innes was drafted into the stand-off role at short notice and John Gallagher earned a recall to the venue of his infamous spear tackle incident two years earlier, primarily to take up the goal-kicking mantle. He had actually been injured in an Alliance game on the Friday night and would have been rated as doubtful but he had declared himself fit when he realised there was another first team opportunity and to his credit did not let anybody down.

Sitting in the stand offered me the opportunity to view the game from a different angle and I was particularly impressed by the committed opening and early score from Gary Mercer that rewarded the good field position that had been gained. Steve Molloy continued in his rich vein of form, ably assisted by Shaun Wane, and both were involved in interpassing to set up the opening for Gary's try and for a minute I thought I was watching Brian Lockwood! Sloppy defensive marking allowed Saints back in the game and although their third try was hotly disputed, in my view Gary Connolly did not knock on before kicking through although whether Alan Hunte forced the ball down over the try line was much more debatable. The referee appeared unsighted and relied upon his touch judge who gave the try to the amazement of even the Saints fans near me. The Leeds scrambling defence around their own line in the second half was a credit to the boys and their fitness and we certainly carved out several chances with close support play without ever getting more than two great penalty goals to bring us back level in the later stages. The game as a whole swung from end to end and was a terrific cup tie that deserved to end in a draw. We were all starting to look forward to a mid-week replay at Headingley before Tea Ropati, who had already missed some easy shots at goal, put over the match-winning drop goal from forty yards out, sending the ball somewhere on to the M6. The defeat was unfortunate and possibly even undeserved but there is no consolation in knowing that you have contributed to a great game and a fine advert for the sport if you have lost. I would rather play boring football and win, especially in a cup tie and the cost of losing to the club as a whole was enormous. Apart from the obvious glory the directors of all the top clubs budget at the start of the season on having good cup runs and plan their finances accordingly, particularly if home league games are sparse at the time.

I had daily monitoring of the injury consisting primarily of intensive treatment and light running and tried to extend myself as far as I could without pain. I progressed to high knee stepping exercises and jogging combined with megapulse, friction and ultrasound physiotherapy and ice packs on the affected area in order to protect the muscles and fibres from further damage. The medical supervision at Headingley under physio Stuart Walker is excellent and as that sort of injury can take anything up to six weeks to fully mend and be as strong it is important to undertake the right tests before rushing back. Knowing relatively early on that I would be missing the next match allowed me some extra time to concentrate on some of the extraneous off-field activities that make up a full-time rugby player's duties. These included such things as answering all my fan mail and organising a programme of events for and attending training with the Leeds Junior Section, the Blue and Amber Club of which I am fortunate enough to be President. I like reading and hearing people's opinions and keeping in touch with the ground swell of support on the terraces although being a family man I do not have time to go talent spotting or watching the amateur game. My priority was to get fit as quickly as possible rather than work specifically in team affairs and in that respect there was little point in trying to confuse or influence Craig Innes with the subtleties of stand-off play. It was more important for him to acquaint himself with the names and calls of the various moves we practise and to work with Andy Gregory. By standing apart you can learn a lot about management and coaching techniques and where best you can make a contribution when hopefully graduating to that position.

Hull (Away) - Stones Bitter Championship 15/11/92

For the return to the Boulevard I decided to obtain a different perspective and elected to stand behind the posts just to the left of the main body of Leeds fans, amongst a group of good-humoured Hull supporters. They treated me with far less malice and vitriol than if I had been out on the pitch and several were genuinely interested to know if I had been approached to return during the summer. The first half effort by the boys was again impressive and possibly the most hard working and effective of the season to date. They grafted well and showed great resilience at a ground where it is never easy to play open football and having gained a 7-0 half-time lead, Hull had never looked in with a chance. What had looked like plain sailing for us changed with a couple of stupid errors right from the restart, including giving away a penalty try that served to put ourselves under enormous pressure. The Hull crowd started to get behind their favourites and we let a winning situation slip away. The injury jinx had already struck again by then with the loss of the influence, pace and inspiration of Alan Tait and it seemed that controversial refereeing decisions were also following us around when we had a perfectly good try that would have given us an 11-6 lead disallowed for a forward pass. After that, we fell into the trap of playing thoughtless football once we had gone behind by surrendering possession and passing at the wrong time. The side showed a lot of character to claw their way back into the match with a spectacular length-of-the-field try only to concede an elementary score from poor marker defence immediately afterwards. That was particularly galling to watch as it is an aspect we spend a lot of time on and work hard at in training and to allow Lee Jackson to go unchallenged from twenty-five yards out was criminal. I can imagine what must have been said about that in the dressing-room at full-time, a situation made worse when it was reported that there was a water failure and the teams had to share a shower.

That defeat marked our sixth in the league from only nine starts, the benchmark by which most good judges evaluate the likelihood of being involved in the destiny of the Championship and meant that effectively we were out of the running and that also we were still looking for our first away win of the campaign. The target would now have to be to get a roll on and win as many games as possible in order to finish hopefully in the top four for a home Premiership tie and to wreck the aspirations of some of the other main contenders.

I made my appearance on *Boots 'n All* the next evening and, even though I was in London and could have gone, I had not received an invitation to the *Panasonic Sports Personality Awards* covered by ITV. That the Great Britain Rugby League Captain had not been acknowledged was bad enough but what made it worse was that the England Rugby Union side received the top team award for winning a Grand Slam and remaining undefeated against some very poor sides, whilst we did not even get a mention. If people are looking for the best all-round side in any sport over the last few years, what have Wigan done wrong not to receive a nomination and some fair recognition? I have got nothing against Rugby Union, in fact I had attended my first live game as a guest of one of the sponsors for the North versus South Africa game at Elland Road, although for most of the time I was watching I was surprised by the lack of action.

That week, the England squad was announced for the forthcoming revived international against Wales at Swansea and I was fortunate enough to be named as captain although this time I had not had any advance notice. It marked another great honour for me as one of only two England players to survive from the last encounter in 1984. The game offered Malcolm Reilly a chance to bring in a crop of new, in-form players and to develop them at a higher standard than that which they were used to. The only way that they will learn and improve is in exactly that sort of environment. Looking at the respective sides it was obvious that Wales were going to be highly motivated and no pushover and that they had picked some class players even in Jonathan Davies's absence which would guarantee that the match would be faster and more vigorous than the majority of Championship fixtures. I was hoping that it would be a success both on and off the pitch and saw it as a forerunner of a regular three match series between the sides akin to the "State of Origin" in Australia, and to provide the stepping stone up to the rarefied demands of Test football. The England side trained together on the Wednesday after it was announced and I went down to Swansea with Malcolm, League Public Affairs Executive David Howes and Geoff Keith to promote the game. Having spoken to the Welsh people and media down there, we knew they were looking forward to a terrific occasion and a partisan atmosphere which fired us all up with anticipation and promised a great experience. The game as a whole can only get better with fixtures of this kind in the schedule and they provide the ideal build-up for the next series of confrontations against our Antipodean rivals.

Chapter Eight

England Expects

The following day we continued our media awareness campaign in Wales and accompanied by Kevin Ellis and Welsh coach Clive Griffiths attended a lunch in the Rhondda in honour of John Bevan who hailed from the area. From what I had been led to believe, the Welsh do not take too kindly to the English on their home soil but this was a new experience for me and I found from their welcome that such stereotypes could not be further from the truth. The lunch was a tremendous success with over five hundred guests and several passionate recollections, a most enjoyable occasion during which we met a few of the old stars from both codes such as Tommy David, Phil Bennett and Dai Watkins. I sought out Steve Fenwick whom I had opposed in my inaugural season for Hull when he had been part of the Cardiff Blue Dragons and it was great to have a chat and reminisce with him again. It was a particularly emotional reunion for John, which we were made to feel very much a part of. There was a strange sensation of not leaving the country for an international fixture and yet quite obviously being the away side and a few of the England players had already enquired as to whether passports would be necessary. We knew all the Welsh boys from our league encounters and I knew how much the event meant to them and their identity. Having visited the venue, the Vetch Field in Swansea which is a great little compact ground, it was not difficult to imagine the atmosphere and intensity that would be generated by a patriotic full-house.

On returning to Leeds to prepare for the game at bottom club Leigh, I knew that I would have to play in order to prove my availability for England. I probably needed more than a fortnight off to regain one hundred per cent fitness but if I had not played then I am sure that Leeds would have been forced to withdraw me from the England squad as a precaution. It was a bit of a risk, especially as the torrential rain leading up to the match dictated that conditions would be at their most testing.

Leigh (Away) - Stones Bitter Championship 22/11/92

Although they had just beaten St. Helens at home to secure their first win of the season, we knew that the match at Hilton Park offered us a real chance of our opening away win of the season. However, we had no intention of underestimating Leigh as it was always a hard tussle over there in an intimidatory setting on a small ground with sparse facilities. The pitch was like a quagmire and not ideal to suit my or Andy Gregory's passing game. We dropped a few balls early on, perhaps trying to be over-ambitious, and it became obvious that the outcome would be dictated by the forwards and who controlled the ball best. There was little doubt that the restricted mobility and the lack of footing in the cloying mud was a great leveller and the incessant rain made handling a lottery. Leigh certainly adapted better than we did even after we had taken an early lead. Without any disrespect to them I am sure that if we had played on a dry ground we would have scored thirty or forty points but we were drawn into a confrontation up the middle and surrendered the initiative to their enthusiasm. Our game plan remained to try and get the ball wide to the centres as early as possible to create some damage but somewhere along the way we got lost in doing the basics and bogged down in the wrong parts of the field and increasingly impatient. Leigh made the most of their chances with a fortunate kick through and we were again looking at a defeat that would have provided the critics with further ammunition. In the end, some inspired combination play from first Kevin Iro and then Craig Innes provided a long-distance try for Carl Gibson that salvaged a point, although Leigh, probably justifiably, felt unfortunate at not winning.

We had to review the result as a point gained rather than surrendered and, perhaps surprisingly in such heavy going, I suffered no reaction or recurrence of the hamstring pull. Despite having missed a couple of matches, fitness and stamina did not prove a problem either as running became almost impossible and the primary role of the half backs became one of merely handing the ball on rather than creating and organising like we should do, whilst Leigh's plan of condensing the play was to suit their strengths and was well executed. The try that earned the point was another spectacular length-of-the-field move that proved what we were capable of with the talent in the side and was a foretaste of what we hoped would come with greater consistency. Ultimately, it was a relief not to lose against the bottom side. That would have increased the growing pressure and criticism from all sectors on the directors, management and therefore the players, who were not impervious to the ongoing chants of "What a waste of money!" from the terraces.

That encounter marked the first under the Rugby League's new edicts on holding down and keeping the sides further apart at the play of the ball, although players and referees were given little chance of fully understanding the implications. We were only informed at training on the Saturday morning that the so-called "flopper" had been outlawed and that defences would have to retire an extra five metres. We were told after the match by referee John Holdsworth that he had strictly applied it for Leigh in the first half and Leeds in the second in order to simplify the transition and make the adjustment easier, as much for his benefit as the players. Much was made of the fact that the game would now be faster and consequently fitness standards would have to be raised, but to be honest the requirements to play at the highest levels nowadays are such that the rule changes make little difference to the amount of ground that needs to be covered, irrespective of the actual distance between the teams. With such a short time to prepare for the Leigh encounter all a coach can stress is the need not to give away silly penalties and remain disciplined and to follow the referee back to wherever he goes with the defensive line which is a standard instruction any way.

Due to the impending international selection and the vagaries of the fixture list following our Regal exit, Leeds now had no match for the next three weeks which was a bit of a farce. Players want to be playing every week, especially in the middle of the season and there is only a limited amount of stamina work that can be undertaken in training, the bulk of it having been done in the pre-season period. Full match fitness comes only from playing regular games and by the end of November emphasis should switch mainly to sprint and speed work. A large gap in the programme is hardly ideal at that time and can become very frustrating and make an eventual return to action even more challenging.

Injury disruption following the weekend's games affected the England side after several key players were forced to withdraw, among them Deryck Fox. That meant that my new half-back partner would be Castleford's Mike Ford and this would be the first time that we had played together at any level and he was the fourth scrum half that I had partnered in representative matches. I was looking forward to it as we seemed to 'gel' together quite well during training and Malcolm seemed pleased with the combination. We had a discussion regarding our styles of play with Mike working with the forwards and releasing the ball when I needed it and I knew what I had to do as link man between him and the outside backs. There was no problem with the new faces in the squad fitting in, all the young lads experiencing their first taste of international football were keen to impress Malcolm and test themselves and their obvious potential. We went into camp on the Wednesday night in Wigan and trained at St. Helens the next day before travelling on down to Swansea and arriving at around six in the evening. Being the captain, I had the privilege of a room to myself but the management always make sure that the new lads are in with someone more experienced to make them feel fully part of the set-up. The Welsh selection contained the surprise of David Bishop at hooker for the first time in his career and in only his second match for ten months. Although this was something of a shock, their coach Clive Griffiths made it clear that David had been picked for his motivational value and was not expected to last more than about half an hour. We knew that one of the biggest inspirations for some of the Welsh squad would be to prove to Malcolm that he was wrong in omitting them from the Lions' touring squad and we were under no illusions that they were after our Great Britain jerseys. We were equally determined not to be beaten and embarrassed by a side whom we had taught to play our game.

On the Tuesday evening before leaving Leeds I had hosted an extremely successful "Blue and Amber" meeting with Gordan Strachan as the guest. There were between eighty and ninety kids and a few of their parents present for a light-hearted, non-controversial question and answer session. Gordon is a smashing bloke with whom I have played golf in a few charity tournaments and who has a lot of funny eating habits, his diet revolving mainly around seaweed tablets and bananas. He is an interesting character who was playing at his peak, leading by example and is still ambitious even though he is in his mid thirties. He is a model to professionals in any sport and also a keen supporter at Headingley along with Gary McAllister, thus strengthening the link between the two clubs in the city which is great to see. A lot of our boys follow the fortunes of Leeds United but it is difficult to get to see them play when we are preparing for a match on the following day.

Wales v England - British Coal International 27/11/92

Part of the England game plan was to nullify the expected aggressive opening by the Welsh and win the crowd over early on. Discipline from the kick-off was the key, especially with débutants in the side and talk before the match was of the likelihood of a physical approach from the packs to obtain dominance. We were aware that the code's image was on trial, not only through Sky's large scale promotion but also if we were going to sell the game seriously to the Welsh public and a series of stop-start penalties or brawls and vendettas early on would have detracted from the spectacle. I sat out the last training session at St. Helens as a precaution having suffered a slight hamstring twinge the previous day. After treatment it cleared up sufficiently going into the game although I was not totally fit. Nevertheless, if you are asked to lead your country and are eighty-five or ninety-five per cent able then you are going to take that gamble. I needed a final late fitness test on the morning of the match at the Swansea Rugby Union ground and went along with Lee Crooks who was practising his goal kicking, a role for which he had been brought in after Deryck's withdrawal. I worked with the physio Dave Fevre from Wigan and was cleared to play.

Despite being a soccer venue, the Vetch Field is like a traditional, typical Rugby League ground. The fans are close to the playing area, generating an intimacy and excitement that serves to heighten the tension and enjoyment. As we walked out the reception was tremendous and although I was not nervous, the playing of the national anthems was particularly emotional and it gave me a real tingle hearing the home crowd get behind their boys and the Welsh team singing and openly crying with pride. The effect was one of admiration rather than intimidation and did not prevent us from taking the vital early advantage. There was little point taking on the larger Welsh pack up the middle and the plan was to spread the ball from second or third man out. I played a bit wider and, getting good service from Mike Ford, tried to bring in Richie Eyres between their centres, a role he plays to great effect with Widnes. With Ellery back to his best form and running off the fringes of the ruck we set up a good lead and solid platform before the Welsh hit back with two quick tries that brought the house down. Their fight back did not really worry us as we felt that they had been allowed into the game only though our basic mistakes, mishandling in the wet, giving away needless penalties and dropping off a couple of tackles near our line. Up to that point they had never looked like scoring and Lee Crooks' try on the stroke of half-time to extend our lead seemed to be the killer blow and knocked the stuffing out of them, causing their heads to drop.

Knowing that their forwards would tire in the later stages, we came out firing in the second half. It was revealed after the match that four or five of the Welsh lads had been carrying injuries and went into the game with pain killing injections and that told, as our fitness carried us through and enabled us to exploit the gaps and play some good open football. As the game went on we kept our discipline and organisation and gave some of the young lads like Steve Molloy, Chris Joynt and Dean Busby the space and time to make their mark. I was involved in creating most of the tries, thanks mainly to Mike's effective handling and I enjoyed our partnership. Ironically, I suffered a recurrence of the hamstring problem in injury time when I stooped to collect a low return pass from Ellery for my try but was gratified by the ovation that I got when I left the pitch to ice it immediately afterwards.

It was obvious from the post match interviews and interest that the venture had been a success and a great advert for Rugby League. The gamble of blooding some new talent paid off for Malcolm and augured well for Great Britain's future prospects. The only major disappointments on the horizon were the limited resources and lack of depth in the Welsh squad which, without an injection of some new talent, may see the series temporarily suspended. The Welsh public were extremely knowledgeable and aware of the intricacies of the code and many people at the official reception afterwards were saying how they had been converted to the game because of the constant action and movement. As is traditional down there, they organised a fantastic night for us and as Leeds did not have a game that weekend I was able to avail myself of their generosity and hospitality, finally getting to bed around four thirty in the morning. There were definitely a few sore heads amongst the party the following day as a testimony to the Welsh spirit.

I rarely, if ever, take in a live match if I have a blank weekend although I do follow the game whenever it is on television. I try to spend as much time as possible with my kids when I am not playing or training as it is not the same as speaking to them on the phone all the time when I am away. After I arrived back in Leeds on the Saturday afternoon we had a family tea at the Rugby League Hall of Fame at the Bentley Arms and a bit of fun around the house before I succumbed to the need for an early night.

Chapter Nine

Crisis – What Crisis?

My regular appearance on *Boots 'N All* coincided with the initial draft proposals for the restructuring of the game. The part that concerned me most was the intention to increase the First Division to sixteen teams and thereby subject the top players to even greater demands. Apart from that the timing of it seemed a little incongruous, despite the best efforts of Maurice Lindsay to make his mark as the new Chief Executive. Those instantly affected were the players in the lower divisions who appeared to have their incentives removed mid-season. Such major plans and decisions are better left until the close season for implementation and then everyone, including the spectators, know where they stand. Most pundits seemed to accept that the First Division players were being asked to perform in too many games and that it is not necessarily the League fixtures but the Cup ones that cause the overcrowding problems. The need to obtain and maintain sponsorship for the game, especially during a recession, is vital but it does seem to be the players who suffer for it. Additionally, promoting two extra sides of a lesser quality would not have given any of the top players the greater intensity of competition they needed to progress and match the Australians. My preference would have been for three equal divisions of twelve clubs and for neighbouring sides to merge if they were in difficulties and thereby preserve the sport in that area. With no prospect of an immediate match for Leeds, the training became quite boring and lacking in variation as the priority switched to stamina work to maintain fitness, comprised mainly of endless running which I do not look forward to. By way of compensation, at the weekend Colin Maskill, Dave Creasser and myself as members of the Omnibus Golf Society were able to get in some most enjoyable competition. There were also a couple of "Blue and Amber" Christmas events to co-ordinate which were a great success but hard work trying to control and look after over one hundred children. Steve Molloy made an excellent job of Father Christmas at the party although he needed a couple of days off training afterwards. There were also several coaching sessions for forthcoming curtain raisers. All the events are extremely worthwhile when you see the children smiling and how much they get out of it.

Throughout the enforced break I was having regular treatment and rehabilitation exercises both at the club and the local BUPA hospital where I tried out a revolutionary machine for testing muscle strength and movement. Straight after the England game I had ruled myself out of the next Leeds match at Sheffield in an effort to shake off the nagging injury. At the same time, the opening shots of what was to become an intense debate and controversy were fired by Malcolm Reilly when he criticised top stars who played back-to-back rugby and was quoted in the *Rugby Leaguer* as saying that players do not give their best on their return and need the off season to recover and prepare properly. I did not see the article or speak to him about it but I did hear what he had said. When the opportunity arose, Malcolm himself left the English game when he went to play full time club rugby at Manly for more money than he was offered at Castleford. Whilst that simmered it also appeared that discussions were taking place between Leeds and Wakefield involving me in a possible if unrealistic player swap which was upsetting. I am totally committed to Leeds and I certainly did not appreciate people trying to deal behind my back. I was not able to find out who had initiated it and the reasons for it.

No official from Leeds either confirmed or denied it to me and at no stage did I take part in any negotiations. If there was any sort of problem with me either being a disruptive influence or not doing the job they wanted me to do then I would have gladly discussed it with anyone at Headingley in an effort to sort it out.

Sheffield (Away) - Stones Bitter Championship 13/12/92

When I arrived at the Don Valley Stadium to watch the game, a woman spectator came up to me and said that she had not liked my reference on *Boots 'N All* to Sheffield as a nuisance side capable of causing the odd upset. I did not remember saying that although I must have done for her to mention it and apparently the Sheffield side were also using it as a spur, though I would have thought that the chance to beat Leeds for the first time since their inception would have been a greater one. It is a strange place, a very nice stadium with luxury facilities on one side but really it is too big. The Sheffield fans generate a great atmosphere with their vocal support but they are too far away from the pitch, which itself is quite small once you are out there and I reckon that a more purpose-built rugby arena would suit them.

The Leeds team started out quite well, belying their lay-off and opened up an early 4-0 lead, playing some flowing football and keeping Sheffield in their own twenty-five before falling off the pace and allowing the Eagles to get a roll on and increase in confidence. There seemed to be a tendency under the new laws for players to scoot directly from acting half-back and rely on one-man drives into the opposition and over the advantage line which was not part of the Leeds game plan. There was also evidence of a quicker play of the ball with the elimination of the gang tackling that had previously slowed the game down and Sheffield exploited the need to get back into the line as fast as possible and plug the gaps up the middle. The injury jinx struck again, this time affecting Andy Goodway who broke his arm in the early stages, but that should not have affected the concentration of the players who were left on the park. We again fell into the trap of immediately conceding a try having had one disallowed for a forward pass and instead of being well ahead and in control we surrendered the initiative and territorial advantage. It always takes a short time to recompose yourself after the disappointment of not having a valid looking score allowed and that is when you are at your most vulnerable, especially away from home. Garry Jack's try to extend their lead at half-time stemmed from very poor defence but we battled back and improvised a couple of well-worked tries after the interval to regain the lead before rather alarmingly running out of steam. To concede eighteen points in the last twelve minutes against a very workmanlike, well organised side was very unprofessional and justifiably had people asking where was our team spirit, passion and pride, which did hurt the players. We are only human and do make mistakes but it was very distressing and embarrassing for all connected with the club as the speculation and ridicule increased. The major criticism seemed to centre on the side playing as a group of individuals rather than a team and maybe we were expecting too much of each other as single world class talents rather than playing to a designated pattern and making sure that we had secured the right field position before exploiting our opponents' defensive line with our undoubted range of attacking options.

Losing away from home can become a habit or psychological barrier if you allow it to and possibly induced a measure of panic football into our play but we had no excuses for such a disjointed performance. The media were quick to jump on to the bandwagon and used the result to indicate a measure of crisis at the club. Facts do not lie and with the calibre of players available our league position of third from bottom gave justified cause for complaint. The only answer was more hard work on the training pitch and a need to maintain our self belief and to keep practising what we knew was the right way of playing. Nobody goes out there to play badly and we did not plan to do anything different in our next build up.

That evening saw the BBC Television *Sports Personality of the Year Awards* for which myself, Ellery and Andy Gregory had received invitations. Andy was too disappointed after the Sheffield game and decided not to go, so Ellery and I got into a car and dashed to Leeds and Bradford Airport for the 7.15 flight to London. We arrived there at 8.00 and were at the studio at the Queen Elizabeth Centre in Westminster at nine and so missed most of the programme and all of the coverage of Rugby League. We were only there for forty-five minutes but attended the reception afterwards with the Wigan lads who had been featured and had quite a good night. It was particularly gratifying to mix with Dewi Morris and Simon Hodgkinson from Rugby Union, Ally McCoist and Mark Hateley from Soccer and Graeme Hick and Richard Illingworth from the Cricket world who all expressed their enjoyment of our game, avidly followed the coverage of it and had no difficulty in recognising us.

National exposure for the game continued the next day, with me at the centre of conjecture and speculation after Leeds announced that they had refused permission for me to play for Manly during the off season. I was very upset when the story broke, especially as I had signed a contract in September and during October Leeds' Chief Executive, Alf Davies had spoken to Graham Lowe, the Manly coach, regarding my availability and he had not given any indication that there would be a problem with clearance. Alf told me of the conversation at the time and asked if I had spoken to Graham and I confirmed to him that an approach had been made. I had played almost continuous back-to-back football from when I turned professional in 1983 without any detriment and I could not understand why Leeds had taken such a decision at that time. There was no clause in my contract, which ran from August to May, stating that I could not go although I fully understood the Leeds position and explanation that they wanted me to rest and fully prepare for the next domestic season without being burnt out or jaded. Balanced against that, I would not have accepted the deal if I had thought that it would have been in any way detrimental to my performances for Leeds or Manly and the opportunity further to secure my financial future out of a limited playing career was something I had to consider. If I had thought that I could not handle the situation I would not have agreed in the first place. I am not a cheat and would not have gone to Manly merely to take the money and run or put my Leeds career in jeopardy. I spoke to Manly who were initially prepared to take me on an even shorter term contract from the end of the Leeds' season to the first week in August but my offer of a reduced stint was to no avail. The financial implications meant that I had little option but to take legal advice over the exact terms of my Leeds contract and the possibility of a restraint of trade, as anyone would in that situation but at no stage did I issue a writ or instigate or threaten to take the club to court. I was surprised at the way the whole situation was made public at the outset and I mentioned to Doug Laughton that all the discussions could have taken place behind closed doors and then there would not have been a problem. As it was, it appeared that I was the 'bad boy' and fuelled rumours regarding what my attitude would be towards playing for Leeds and whether I would be totally committed on the pitch. As far as I was concerned nothing had changed in that aspect, Leeds is my club, I love the place and the people and still intend to finish my career there. I never considered the possibility of playing in Australia full-time although I was offered that chance by Balmain in 1985 but now that both my youngsters are settled at school it would have been too much of a disruption even to contemplate.

Despite my obvious disappointment, my appearance on *Boots 'N All* the evening the story broke gave me the opportunity to state my case, as there are always two sides to every disagreement, and to try to defuse the situation a little. There was some speculation that the issue had been brought up as a smoke screen to deflect criticism from Leeds' generally poor start to the season but, like the majority of articles written, that was based more on guesswork and exaggeration rather than truth or fact. The issue did put the subject of twelve month contracts for the top players firmly on the agenda at a time when the game was reviewing itself. That would undoubtedly solve the problem of the drain of our top talent to the Antipodes and was something that I had stressed to Maurice Lindsay on the programme the previous week. There would be no argument from the players if they were contracted to the Rugby League during the summer months, as in Cricket, and we would be available to attend coaching clinics at Lilleshall or the Rugby League Schools of Excellence as Malcolm Reilly had requested he would like to see.

The other major talking point that night was the players' strike at Hull Kingston Rovers over agreed payments during which I reiterated my belief that the creation of a strong Players Association was vital for the game as a whole. I felt sorry both for their spectators, who were denied the chance of seeing their best players in a crucial match, and the players themselves who were at loggerheads with the board but without any form of representation or arbitration. With an effective Players Association those matters could be sorted out behind the scenes without disrupting events on the field.

Back in Leeds at our regular Tuesday team meeting after the Sheffield result its implications were fully discussed. Nobody could put their finger on the reason for the collapse and Doug rightly mentioned that there was little point in singling anyone out for criticism as we were all in the same boat together. His mood of getting on and putting things right in order to get the best out of everyone and to encourage rather than humiliate was taken up by the renewed resolution of the squad. Word got around the club about the Challenge Cup draw and the prospect of playing Barrow at home was a boost to our morale and the signal of a possible change in fortune, particularly as a lot of the other top sides were destined to make an early exit after opposing each other. My discussions with the club regarding the Manly affair were completely separate to concentrating on the next game and did not affect my training or the spirit in the dressing-room. I did not feel that I needed to offer explanations to anyone on that score.

Halifax (Home) - Stones Bitter Championship 18/12/92

The fact that the return match against Halifax was live on Sky gave the side an immediate chance to respond to the criticism and to try to put the record straight even if being under the microscope tended to magnify the pressure. We knew, and had proved, that with the talent at our disposal we could score tries from anywhere against anybody but that our problems were on defence and specifically in our communication. My confrontation opposite Paul Bishop did not worry me as despite his fiery reputation he is not a stand-off. I had the additional pleasure of seeing my daughter lead the side out as our mascot and I was quite surprised how well and confidently she did it, especially as I came out last and I thought that she might have been crying and waiting for me. When I had briefed her about what her duties entailed in walking out with Ellery, running three or four yards and then passing a ball she had said, "I'm not doing that Dad, I'm going to score a try so that you can get a few points on." After the game she complained that the referee had been a little bit stingy. They usually give the mascots a one pound coin but she had only got fifty pence from him and in the end I had to give her an envelope with five pounds in it to keep her quiet. Injuries to Steve Molloy and Shaun Wane meant that we put out a reshuffled pack which against the bigger Halifax six may have caused us problems if we had not spread the ball wide. Our forwards showed a lot of character and refused to be dominated after we had made our customary slow start and allowed Halifax to go 8-0 up. That set the tongues wagging again and it crossed my mind about what people would think when I missed a kick to touch in the opening minutes. Early on we had put ourselves under pressure by trying to throw the ball about like it was a hot potato in the wrong part of the field and not having an organised kick and chase game, but we did not lose sight of our objective and once we had settled down and made a few inroads we hit back and showed what we were best at. It was important to score consecutive tries and meant that we grew in confidence which became the vital factor. The defence seemed to have a better shape which was something we had worked on and our forwards were making the important first up tackles that stopped Halifax's momentum and nullified their half back combination. As with England I played a little wider out in an effort to link up with Paul Dixon and to exploit the damaging runs of Gary Mercer and Ellery rather than the side trying to rely on penetration up the middle. With the new ten metre rule fully operative I was given the space to run at the opposition a bit more and exploit the gaps when they were on the back foot. It may have appeared that we were indecisive over spurning the opportunity to go for goal with a couple of penalties in the first half but we were trying to catch Halifax on the hop and gain some extra yardage which we achieved.

Kevin Iro's long distance score immediately after the break proved to be the turning point and after the euphoria of their early lead, was a blow from which Halifax never recovered. We put on a good, professional hard-working performance, playing to our strengths of getting the ball moving and showed a killer instinct with the successful execution of some of our planned moves that entertained the crowd, gave us all a great deal of enjoyment and satisfaction and started to prove to the rest of the league that Headingley was a place to be feared. I did not feel particularly exhausted after the match despite the lay-off as I was mainly feeding the other runners and doing the organising and ball handling. Adopting the kicking role may have been a risk with a suspect hamstring which had not totally recovered but if I had not been able to do the job the coach wanted then I would not have played. Instead of the usual Christmas pantomime at the club, the players and their children all got together the next afternoon for a buffet, disco and the traditional visit of the man in red.

I entered into further discussions with the club at the start of the Christmas week in an effort to resolve the Manly situation. I did not get a chance to speak directly to the board but their position was communicated in no uncertain terms during a meeting with Doug who said they had no intention of rethinking the position or altering their stance. I outlined my case and he reconfirmed that they thought I had a good enough domestic contract as it was. As both Leeds and the Rugby League had refused to sanction my agreement with Manly then it was obvious that I would not be going. I felt that as a matter of principle it was important to make some sort of stand and not allow myself to be used as a piece of meat. The fact that Manly felt obligated to pull out of the deal meant that there was little chance of finding a compromise solution although I would have been happy to have had a small clause inserted in my contract stating the club's intentions on allowing me to play abroad. I had a chat on the phone with John Devereux at Widnes who was also going through a similar experience regarding a move to the Sea Eagles which was hampered by disagreement between the clubs over insurance cover. At the same time the Wakefield proposal became public knowledge but I did not know who decided to reveal the details or for what purpose. I reaffirmed my devotion to Leeds in an exclusive article, mainly for the supporters' benefit, in the *Yorkshire Evening Post* but again there was no reaction from the management.

The Christmas period is notoriously difficult for professional sports people who have to curtail their celebrations and make further family sacrifices. We are not totally abstemious although it would not make sense to be seen in a pub, but the biggest problem is to control the temptation to eat too much and pick at the food which is constantly available throughout the day. It is easy to go to bed at eight or nine in the evening feeling bloated which is hardly ideal for a mid morning kick off on Boxing Day. Training was mooted for Christmas Day but as there are a lot of family men at the club we said that we preferred not to and had a hard session throughout the week and especially on Christmas Eve to compensate and to try to prepare for the big match encounter with local rivals Castleford. The freezing weather and fog did not stop the Lancashire lads from coming over to train but it did mean that most of the work had to be undertaken inside in the superb gymnasium at Headingley.

Castleford (Home) - Stones Bitter Championship 26/12/92

The Boxing Day tradition, occasion and atmosphere always gets to the players even though it is difficult for the body to adjust to an early start. I was up at 7.30 a.m. thinking about the game and trying to get the movement going. The slight delay to the kick-off to accommodate the huge crowd increased the anticipation and we knew when we warmed up on the pitch itself beforehand, rather than on the cricket field, that there was a tremendous buzz of expectancy about the place and Headingley looked and sounded as it should do. We knew what was expected from us and I was looking forward to opposing Aussie Peter Coyne whom I had never played against before and whose style of trying to keep the ball in play all the time, particularly with his very accurate kicking into the corners, was a bit different from what I was used to facing.

The match seemed to follow a now familiar pattern, an uncompromising start between two evenly matched sides to get the adrenalin flowing, a disallowed Leeds try, another serious injury this time to Carl Gibson and then going behind. Our counter-attack after Castleford's debatable score was devastating and showed what we could do if the opposition were going to hang off our players. Our support play, exemplified by James Lowes' fifty yard try when the Castleford defence were looking to cover Ellery and Paul Dixon, was excellent and our self-belief grew from that. Up to that point Castleford were being touted as the in-form team and the best placed Yorkshire side but once we began living up to our potential we were virtually unstoppable. My understanding with half back partner Andy Gregory was steadily improving as he regained his full match fitness, allowing him to work with the forwards and me to time the passes for our lethal centre combination. You cannot expect the likes of Kevin Iro and Craig Innes to wait for the ball but need to feed it to them often and with a bit of room and they showed what they could do with their handling and running skills when given the space.

Another early try just after the break gave us the control to dominate the proceedings in all departments and exhibit our full repertoire of skills in front of a delighted crowd against top class opponents. I had been confident that things would eventually start coming together and had even accepted a bet with Lee Crooks after the England match that Leeds would win, despite having to give him a fifteen point start, which turned out to be not so much of a gamble after all. We proved that with the right pride and fire we were a side to be reckoned with and capable of destroying anyone. The crowd were superb in getting behind us even when we were losing early on, as they had done against Halifax, and we got great satisfaction from rewarding them with our entertaining play. My try to end the game was a bit of a bonus rather than any meaningful gesture in response to the off-field sagas.

We sat down in the dressing-room afterwards and stressed the danger of complacency. After two resounding home successes to end the year it was easy to forget some of the criticism and start believing that we really were a good bet for the cup. People had said that we had turned the corner after our victory over Widnes but we had flattered to deceive and not won for four matches after that and we were determined to just take things in our stride. Afterwards, the Boxing Day evening celebrations made up for the slightly muted Christmas as we held a traditional large gathering for family and friends at our house which was great fun for all concerned. When 1992 started Leeds had been at the top of the league and on form and we finished it climbing into eighth spot and in a similar vein. In between we had been disappointing, losing out in a major final but still having something to salvage as we entered the new year. Personally that twelve months had been a very proud time and witnessed me captaining Great Britain on tour and in the World Cup Final and leading out England. If I was to have made any resolutions it would have been to try and remain injury free and to do whatever was necessary for the success of Leeds and Great Britain if Malcolm Reilly wanted me.

A study in kicking technique I - hoisting a bomb for the chasers.
(Credit - Martin Robson)

A study in kicking technique II - concentrating on finding touch.
(Credit - Andy Howard)

Chapter Ten

Turning the Corner

The heralding of 1993 brought little respite in respect of the continuing speculation that Leeds were on the verge of making a major signing. There was little doubt that the squad still needed strengthening by the addition of a couple of recruits but the players are never privy to the team building plans and instead often wonder about the security of their place, which can either act as an impetus or be unnerving, depending on their determination and character. About half of what could be termed the first choice side were almost guaranteed their places on the team sheet whilst some of the others may have felt threatened. If Leeds had still been in with a realistic chance of the Championship then I am sure that signings would have been essential, in particular a versatile middle back and another prop forward. As it was, the market was stagnant and any indication of a possible Leeds interest inflated the asking price and there seemed to be precious little genuine talent available anyway to make a bid for.

Following the clash with Castleford, Andy Gregory had been under an injury cloud all that holiday week and it came as no great surprise when he had to withdraw from the New Year's Day fixture. His replacement, Gareth Stephens, had filled in for him during training and knew the moves to call and the type of half-back partnership I preferred to play, even though his style and game is completely different to Greg's. Unlike for the fans, New Year's Eve is not a particularly celebratory time for the players and I retired at about 7.30 in the evening in order to be prepared for the game rather than watch the calendar change. There was some reassurance in the next day's *Yorkshire Evening Post* when Dougie Laughton stated in his weekly column that he never let good players go, let alone class ones, and I hoped that in the light of those remarks that my name would now stop being mentioned in any transfer discussions as the cup deadline for signings approached.

Salford (Home) - Stones Bitter Championship 1/1/93

The match against the Red Devils pitched me against one of the new breed of aspiring professionals with a bright future in the game, Steve Blakeley, whom Salford had recently signed from the Wigan Alliance team. I had seen him briefly on the television and there is no doubt that behind a dominant pack he would be a class act. He has all the attributes required of a half-back with great vision, an ability to read and support play as well as being a reliable kicker. Despite the match being Salford's first competitive game after an enforced month's lay off which made a mockery of the fixture list, we had no plans to put them under extra pressure early on in the hope that they would tire quickly and buckle. We knew that a patient build-up was vital and that we had to work to gain the openings rather than throw caution to the wind. During the warm up for any game we always assess and discuss the playing conditions and we realised that the choice of ends would be important as there was a high, bright late-afternoon sun that we thought might have been a disadvantage to play into during the first half. Fortunately, Ellery won the toss and that allowed us to prove the point. Like Halifax and Bradford before them, the Salford side contained a large ex-Leeds contingent with Craig Coleman, Phil Ford, David Cruikshank, David Young and Rob Ackerman all in their squad and eager to perform well at the home of their old club.

We created and bombed a lot of early chances to get points on the board but we did not feel that we needed to change the pattern of play and we did eventually manage to break down Salford's organised defence and take the lead. In most of our previous matches we had tried to rush things in the opening quarter, usually paid the penalty by falling behind and then had to rely on our class players to dig us out of the hole. We may well have been lulled into a false sense of security because having extended our advantage we started to get in each other's way a bit on attack, with some of the players trying to improvise around our game plan in an effort to get themselves on the score sheet. Our defensive intensity seemed to slacken off and lead to us conceding a try at the worst possible time, right on the stroke of the interval – that should have proved a warning. Even though we knew we had their measure, we allowed Salford back into the match straight after the resumption when we fell for another dummy near the line to give away a further try and the lead. That galvanised us and as we regrouped behind the posts we realised that we were in for a game and put the last half hour into perspective. The transformation paid immediate dividends as we upped our work rate and began a series of punishing raids that led to a try for Ellery which allowed us to dominate proceedings and proved again what we were capable of once we started concentrating. The satisfaction of our late points flourish was tempered by the knowledge that we had yet to sustain that effort for the full eighty minutes which would be crucial against the top sides. In that final quarter, after our forwards had gained an impressive platform for the backs with some good clearing runs and quick play the balls, we exhibited some ruthless finishing by coming on to the ball from depth and getting on the outside of the defenders. The pace and strength of wingers Jim Fallon and Simon Irving was particularly effective and their determined scores in the corners delighted the Headingley faithful and maintained the finest traditions of wing play to which they had become accustomed.

Despite a resounding score line we knew that there were still important aspects of our organisation that needed working on if we were to achieve an away win and build on three consecutive victories. I was as surprised to win Man of the Match award as were the crowd, who booed and jeered the announcement, and I laughed at the time as I knew that neither I nor any member of my family had made the decision. Afterwards, I did get annoyed when I heard people commenting that it was a sweetener for not being allowed to go to Manly and as a counter to the transfer talk. The mood was positive in the dressing-room as we knew that the Christmas period was always going to be a crucial one for the outcome of the season. We had said all along that with the new blood in the side it would take us until then to 'gel' together and know each other's strengths and we had come through the period unbeaten and scoring an average of forty points a game. There was no doubt that the players' confidence was coming back and that we were seeing the basis of a settled side, both of which were crucial elements for continued success.

The run of three stylish home victories was important not only for the belief of the side but also as a reward for the devotion of the long-suffering spectators. During a successful run if some of the players are carrying knocks they tend to declare themselves available even if they are only seventy-five per cent fit in order to maintain their form and not risk losing their place. Ultimately though, the coach knows what each of the players is capable of and that contribution to the overall team effort is paramount. The determination and pressure to achieve our first away victory was starting to prey on our minds and was next tested at Wilderspool in a match brought forward at short notice to Friday night for coverage on Sky. The relatively late decision did not really affect our training pattern or disrupt our match preparations. In many ways I prefer the occasional Friday night match because they leave the weekends free for a more normal social life. The media were beginning to take notice of our true potential rather than enjoy knocking us while we were down and in some cases were in danger of going from one extreme to the other by tipping us as likely Challenge Cup winners rather than candidates for relegation, which was a little bit premature. My appearance on *Boots 'N All* coincided with the postponement of the plans for the restructuring of the sport and the decision to leave things as they were and I was relieved to see that good sense had finally prevailed and that the game's Board of Directors had saved face.

The fact that Warrington had won at Wigan three days before our meeting meant that not only would they be buoyant but that we would have to treat them with the utmost respect. Initially we had thought that they might be feeling the effects of that encounter and that Wigan would have picked them off and that their confidence would be low. Having seen them turn a strong Wigan side over we were very much on our mettle, knowing that games over there were normally uncompromising at the best of times. Prior to the match, as the transfer deadline became ever nearer, speculation was still rife that I was in the middle of a convoluted swap deal involving Jonathan Davies moving from Widnes to Leeds and me swapping places with Ian Lucas at Wigan. I only ever read about such rumours in the press and did not really know what was going on. I was sure that in the absence of any major moves on the horizon that certain journalists searching for a good story were looking at the strengths and weaknesses of the top sides and were inventing their own most likely scenario before seeking confirmations or denials. What annoyed me more than anything was that people were stopping my parents and family in the streets and pubs and asking them if there was any truth in it all, which put them in a difficult position.

Warrington (Away) - Stones Bitter Championship 8/1/93

The arrangements for an evening kick-off in Lancashire do not vary very much from our normal routine. The only real difference is in personal preparation and in having to hang about during the day waiting for the match. I took my daughter to school before lazing about the house and then going back to bed in the early afternoon to relax in order to keep my mind on the job. We assembled at Headingley at 4.00 p.m. before travelling across to the Novotel at Swinton to pick up the Lancashire lads and stop for hot or soft drinks. There was the boost of Andy Gregory returning to the side when it looked as though he might have missed this game; his influence was always going to be important at one of his old clubs. I have always enjoyed playing at Wilderspool which has some excellent facilities, a good pitch and a great atmosphere generated by the spectators who are close to the play and who make themselves heard. I had first played there when I was thirteen for Yorkshire Schoolboys and the ground holds some good memories for me.

It was important to get a good start and we saw plenty of the ball in the opening minutes that enabled us to score a well-worked try from a blind side move. We really built on that effort and to find ourselves at 18-0 up after only twenty minutes and everything coming off was an amazing feeling and not something I had ever experienced before over there. It seemed as though the game was going to be a walk-over but again our concentration lapsed and we started to play over-elaborate touch and pass type football in the wrong parts of the field and using the wrong players, which allowed the Wire back into the game with two tries just before the break, both as a result of our own mistakes. During the talk at half-time we never contemplated shutting the game down and holding on to the lead we had but we still had to be wary of underestimating Warrington's resilience. Some of the lads thought that they might weaken after ten or fifteen minutes of the second period following their midweek exertions but I pointed out that if they did manage to score again then there was no way that with the character in their side they would tire and that we really had to go at it for the full forty minutes. Warrington were certainly fired up and in confident mood for the crucial opening exchanges of the second half and a bit more niggle crept into the game in an effort to break the deadlock. I got Paul Cullen's knees in my back after a tackle and when I had recovered and asked him why he had done it he assured me that it was as a mark of respect! Even though we appeared to be in the driving seat, we never really took complete control of the match even after I had scored an interception try when taking a pass from my opposite number, Kevin Ellis, who did not have the best of nights. We were good mates on the tour and I thought that it must have been a repayment for all the drinks he owed me. I winked at him as I jogged past after converting the try and he gave me a vicious drop dead look which I thanked him for in the bar afterwards. At 30-14 ahead that should have signalled the end of the resistance but Warrington never gave up, showed a lot of spirit, took their chances and by the final whistle we were lucky to hang on for the win which in the end came down to Simon Irving's successful goal kicks. We lost far too much possession in the closing stages through Warrington raking the ball back at the play the ball which was something we had stressed to be aware of in our team meetings.

My drop goal in the final minute which secured our first away win was a great relief for everyone associated with the club, but even that should have happened on the previous play. We had again been in danger of becoming victims of our own flamboyant football and nearly surrendered a match which we should have dominated after such an impressive opening. The closeness of the sides in the middle of the league was illustrated by the fact that the win took us temporarily into fourth place in the table when only three weeks earlier we had been third from bottom. The realisation of that possibility before the match had given us an extra incentive and a measure of satisfaction afterwards that we had started to turn things around.

With the weekend off I had the chance to prepare for my appearance on *A Question of Sport* which was recorded on the Sunday evening in Manchester.

I had received a phone call during December asking me if I would like to go along and represent the code on the BBC television quiz. I was delighted to accept although I did not do any specific research beforehand even though I do not have an extensive range of sporting knowledge, just what I pick up through the papers and on television. I got a fair amount of stick from my friends in the local pub when they heard as they continually doubted my intelligence. I did not know until I arrived which team I would be on and I asked David Coleman who informed me that I was on Ian Botham's side, although several of my friends had hoped it would be Bill Beaumont's. It is a general entertainment show and a lot of fun but there is still a competitive element between the teams and certainly neither captain enjoyed being beaten in their sporting careers. I took my father, brother and a friend along for moral support and it was a great experience for them to meet the other celebrities at the welcome buffet although unfortunately we could not get near Chris Eubank because of the close attention of his rather large minder. I was very nervous beforehand, knowing that about seven or eight million people would eventually be watching, but I was put at ease by Ian Botham who told me not to worry if I got anything wrong. Some of my early fears were dispelled by David Coleman who, when introducing the teams, announced the captains as Bill Botham and Ian Beaumont! I realised that if such an old pro was prone to the odd mistake then I had little to worry about. The programme took between one and a half and two hours to record and none of the questions or categories were pre-planned. I really enjoyed the whole experience and we all mixed in the hospitality suite afterwards where Ian, Bill and David Coleman were very complimentary and knowledgeable about Rugby League. In the final analysis not only was I on the winning side but I managed to get all my own questions right. I did not think that I had let anyone down and I would love the opportunity to appear again in the future.

The transfer deadline expired at midday on January 11th without any major moves, which was an indication of how the recession was affecting the game. That put an end to most of the theorising if not the leaking of rumours to the press which seemed to stem from sources outside of the clubs or the players concerned. Despite the fact that we had won four games on the trot and broken the away hoodoo, training did not become any more relaxed or less intense, if anything it got a little harder in order to combat any likelihood of complacency. That was always likely to be a problem with the return match against Salford coming up within the space of a fortnight and was another example of the poor fixture planning that was afflicting the season. It is extremely hard for players to remain motivated when meeting the same opposition and even more difficult for the respective coaches, especially the vanquished one, who had little time to analyse the videos and alter the game plans to suit. At Headingley we suddenly had the additional unfair pressure of trying to cope with the raised expectations of our supporters and the media writers who were now beginning to expect us to win with a points spree which was unrealistic, especially when playing away from home. Points are a by-product of the correct execution of the game plan, the intention is first and foremost to win. As an added impetus to the side the game marked the début of one of the crop of emerging youngsters at the club when Graham Middleton took his place in the second row. All the senior professionals rallied round to make his introduction easier and even though he had been around for three years serving his apprenticeship in the reserves it is always hard to take the step up even at training, the pace of which was much harder than he was used to. We tried to settle him down and told him not to try to do too much but to concentrate on what he did best, especially on defence.

In an effort to finally defuse all talk of me being unsettled at the club and to get a definitive reaction from the management, I used my column in *Yorkshire On Sunday* to appeal for clarification of my position which was turned into headline news and provoked much comment amongst the supporters. The main reason for the article, which was at my instigation

107

and not the editor's, was to stop my family from being hounded and to assure the public that none of the events or intimations had anything to do with me. I wanted to know where I stood with the Leeds Board and Staff. I knew that at a club like Leeds there would always be rumours circulating and that was accepted but as I was one of the top players, both the fans and I needed some assurances.

Salford (Away) - Stones Bitter Championship 17/1/93

The Willows is my favourite away ground, the dressing-rooms may be amongst the worst but it is a nice, relaxed atmosphere, a wide and long pitch and the Salford public have always been very sporting towards the Leeds players. I had never been in a beaten side there since signing for Leeds and I always looked forward to the trip. The surface on this occasion was very sandy which is always a worry for the players as the heavy going takes its toll on your legs and often leads to fatigue early on in a match and the need to dig in and call on all your reserves of energy. We opened up with the intention of trying to run the Salford pack around by throwing the ball about as they had played in a crucial midweek relegation battle with Leigh. Equally important, our defence early on was quite tight and in numbers and our field kicking and chase were very effective. Even after they had taken an early lead our response was immediate with Graham Middleton heavily involved in Gary Mercer's try with a beautiful round-the-man pass which a seasoned international would have been proud of, never mind a débutant, and which settled his nerves. We managed to conjure up a number of chances and spectacular tries from distance using our various attacking skills and set move options, especially as the Salford defence could not contain the pace of our powerful centres, Craig Innes and Kevin Iro. The quality scores were a fitting reward for our hard work at training and we dictated the game by playing to our strengths.

There was a disconcerting period of about ten minutes in the second half when we again stepped off the gas to allow Salford a couple of soft, sloppy scores. Up to that point we had seemed to be continually on the attack and going the length of the field from the kick-offs with our forwards busting up the middle which until then had not been their strong suit. Salford gave us the space to work in which we capitalised on and even though we scored nine tries we knew that there were still aspects to work on to produce an even better, more balanced eighty minute performance. I had two tries disallowed for forward passes which I was annoyed about at the time, but forty-six points away from home was not a bad return.

On the burst at Salford, a happy hunting ground. *(Credit - Graham Clay)*

Toying with the opposition. *(Credit - Martin Robson)*

Chapter Eleven

The Cup Challenge

My article in *Yorkshire On Sunday* prompted a response from Alf Davies, the Chief Executive of Leeds, who on the radio after the match and in print the next day made a categorical statement that I was contracted to Leeds until 1995 and hopefully for longer. No one actually reiterated that to my face or confirmed it to me directly which was a pity, but I expected that signalled the end of the matter. I would have liked the opportunity to hear the views and plans of the football committee and to restate my intentions to finish my playing career at Headingley and hopefully start a coaching role there.

Another quirk in the ill thought out fixtures gave us a further week's break when our most lucrative home match against Wigan was cancelled as they were in the Regal Trophy Final. On the back of our mounting unbeaten run we would have quite fancied and been ready to take on the champions and it was a compliment to the way we were playing that Widnes turned down the chance of a rearranged fixture at Naughton Park as they did not want to meet us after their own midweek game, even with home advantage. Maintaining continuity can become difficult when only playing on alternate weeks, but the lure of Wembley and the magic of the Challenge Cup was now in focus. The public imagination was undoubtedly captured by the competition and talk centred on how many points they thought we would run up against Third Division opponents, Barrow. Such constant talk can put the players into a false sense of security and give them a feeling of invincibility without putting in the necessary effort. Without being disparaging about our Cumbrian foes we knew that we would win the tie even if we did not play to the peak of our form, but of more concern was the growing body of opinion that this would be our year and that, even before kicking off for the first round, pundits like Mike Stephenson on Sky were predicting that we would lift the trophy. If the players and particularly the backroom staff had started to believe that hype then we were in danger of again ending up with egg on our faces.

Barrow (Home) - Silk Cut Challenge Cup 31/1/93

We knew very little about our opponents other than that they were struggling to find any sort of consistency and that they seemed to have a leaky defence. It was strange to think that the match was our first at home on a Sunday for three months and the main talking point on the terraces was the coupon odds that gave Barrow a seventy point start which was virtually unheard of. In a way, that put us in a no-win situation but at the end of the day our only concern was to be in the draw for the next round. I had first played against my opposite number, Steve Rea, when I was an amateur turning out for Yorkshire against Cumbria and since then he had not had a lot of luck or the best of times in his professional career.

As with the majority of matches in any sport against teams from a lower division who view the encounter as their final, the standard tends to be played at the lowest common denominator. We seemed to get dragged down to Barrow's level and drawn into their game and surprisingly gave them a 6-0 lead when Andy Gregory presented them with a gift interception try. We never gave a thought to the possibility of there being a shock on the cards and we knew we could switch on the tries whenever we needed to as we did in a purple patch just after half time. The pitch was heavy and acted as a levelling factor as we had been training on very solid ground and the softer surface took it out of us no matter how well we had prepared. I picked up a knee injury early on when twisting on the yielding turf and was wary of it throughout the match. I had strained the medial ligaments in my left knee a couple of years before which had kept me out of the game for four weeks and, although this one was not as serious, I knew that I had to try and keep the joint moving or it would stiffen up immediately. I tried to run it off and there was ice waiting in the dressing room at half-time in an effort to control and limit the extent of the damage.

Barrow took every opportunity to slow the game down especially at the play the ball and continually stood offside to stifle any flow in the play which was understandable and the sort of tactics we were expecting. We failed to get deep enough on attack in general play to counter those measures and spilled too much possession on the early tackles following scrums to really run riot. In reality, Barrow got in our way and successfully limited our edge. The introduction of young prop Paul Anderson with his straight power running at the heart of their defence gave us direction and enabled us to go forward rather than just rely on cross-field passing for its own sake. His hard yardage charges sucked the Barrow tacklers in and gave us the space to exploit the gaps as they tired. The result was never in any doubt but I did not enjoy the game which for most of the Leeds players became boring to play in. That was translated into our patchy overall performance which still brought us over fifty points but we were annoyed at the unprofessional way that we had given away eighteen. Had we been playing against stiffer opposition we would have been under much greater pressure and possibly paid the ultimate penalty for our lapses.

I knew straight after the game that I was going to have a problem with my knee and that I was always going to be doubtful for the next match. Whilst I waited to assess the full extent of the injury and for the swelling to subside, I made the national sporting headlines the morning after following comments picked up in my Sunday column that the England Rugby Union team were boring. I had watched the incessant hype before their game with the French and then sat through the match which for me had been less than inspiring. All the stars were out there but were so under-utilised by the tactics employed that someone like Rory Underwood might as well have been sitting next to me on the settee watching the game on the television. The commentators and analysts were continually saying what a marvellous, exhilarating game it was but I just could not see it as a spectacle. Rather than being disparaging about another sport, my aim was to appeal for recognition of Rugby League on its merits and for our code to get an equal treatment, publicity and coverage. I knew that probably would never happen and that the Rugby Union internationals would always generate an atmosphere and occasion irrespective of the product on offer. The remarks must have ruffled a few feathers however as they were apparently picked up by Radio Five and made into a news story and commented upon during the day, which I had not realised at the time. A lot of people I knew told me that they thought the points made were justified and fairly represented a growing body of opinion but not everyone, even within Rugby League, shared or agreed with them, although I defended my right to say them. I even reiterated an offer for the Great Britain Rugby League team to play the England Rugby Union team in a charity match under any rules, which was an idea first proposed by Maurice Lindsay in 1990 when he was trying to promote the First Test against the Aussies at Wembley during a publicity lunch in London that was attended by several leading Rugby Union correspondents. It was meant as a realistic challenge, although I am sure that it will never happen, mainly because everyone knows that there could only be one winner.

The cup draw was again kind to us, two of our chief rivals, Wigan and Saints were paired together and we received another welcome home draw, this time against Second Division Rochdale. I was on the edge of my seat watching it as all the big boys were still available when our number came out of the bag and it was a great relief to avoid them. I was very interested to see Harry Jepson's face as he officiated at the draw, for as well as being a Leeds director he is also on the League's board and afforded himself the grin of a Cheshire cat when the two Lancashire giants came out as the tie of the round.

The following evening the *A Question of Sport* that I appeared in was transmitted. Up until that time I had steadfastly refused to divulge the outcome of the contest or how I had fared. I had undertaken to arrange a charity match between my local pub side, the Omnibus in Belle Isle, and the Leeds Supporters in aid of David Creasser's testimonial fund and after a coaching session with the pub lads we finished in time to watch the programme together, which I really enjoyed. I took the usual barrage of insults and mickey-taking from them but in the end they seemed pleased that I had not let myself, them, or the game as a whole down and emerged with some credit. My earlier comments on the state of Rugby Union took an ironic twist later that week when Wasps full-back Steve Pilgrim was banned for a year by the Union authorities for having an unpaid trial in our Alliance side. The whole episode seemed incredibly petty and unjust in trying to prevent a player from bettering himself.

I left the decision on whether to play at Hull KR until the last minute and only withdrew after training on the Saturday morning as a precaution as I could have played if there had been no alternative. The team had trained for most of the preceding week with Andy Gregory and Gareth Stephens as the half-back combination and so it was not a major set-back to the side and did not upset the rhythm. It was important to get our thoughts off the prevailing cup fever and keep our minds on consolidating our league position and remain ahead of the chasing pack and in contention for a top four place. We knew that with the increasing parity of all the teams we could not take anything for granted after our mini revival. The fact that players of all clubs knew that they had to be on their guard no matter who

117

they faced maintained tremendous interest in the season as whole.

Hull Kingston Rovers (Away) - Stones Bitter Championship 7/2/93

There is something disconcerting about New Craven Park, the purpose built home of Hull Kingston Rovers, which is situated on the edge of the city in a wilderness opposite a cemetery. The dressing-rooms and showers are spacious in contrast to the pitch which was in a terrible state and had been brought in by at least five yards to the legal minimum for this clash, in an effort to counter our advantage and pace out wide. Whilst their side was relatively young and contained no obvious stars it was very workmanlike and we knew that they had great spirit and would work well for each other and their respected coach George Fairbairn, even if they were short of that vital ingredient of experience.

The decision to play Andy Gregory at stand-off surprised a few people but we did not really have a lot of choice having already released Carl Grigg who had covered for me at Sheffield. The other alternative, to move Craig Innes to number six would have meant splitting up our most effective centre combination which would have blunted our attacking options. The lads got a good start with some imposing, solid defence in the early period and a good try from Kevin Iro that augured well and was just what we needed before we again went off the boil. By not respecting possession we were on the defensive for long periods in our own quarter and scrambling to make numerous consecutive tackles before the break. The team allowed some inconsistent refereeing decisions to affect them, especially as a number of them felt that we had been made to turn the ball over on the fifth tackle instead of the sixth prior to Hull Kingston Rovers' opening score. That kind of thing can affect players at the time, but the only thing that is certain is that the officials are not going to change their minds no matter how justified or vociferous the protests. The second half became scrappy and punctuated by penalties before Alan Tait's sin-binning, (which was surprisingly for a remark made by Andy Gregory), seemed to act as a stimulus and we finally raised our game to compensate for his temporary loss. As the match moved into the last ten minutes, it looked as though an amazing blunder by Vince Fawcett under our posts would gift the game to the Robins but we showed a lot of character and resilience to retain our nerve and create the space for Gareth Stephens to crash over out wide to seal a late victory with his first try for the club. It was a measure of our progress that we would have undoubtedly lost that match if it had been played earlier in the season and we again proved that if we worked for the full eighty minutes we could come up with the right result, although Hull KR would probably have felt aggrieved at the outcome. The general consensus of opinion amongst the players and, from what I could hear, from the supporters, was that any away win was valuable as were the accompanying two points. We had managed to salvage and maintain our winning run which was becoming an enjoyable habit and a continued boost to our confidence.

Having achieved a measure of consistency in our performance that had been sadly lacking earlier on in the campaign, we returned to the cup trail and looked forward to the tie against Rochdale and hopefully a convincing victory and a relatively straightforward passage into the quarter finals. Being mid-table Second Division opponents, the build up was inevitably low key, especially as all the media interest focused on the televised clash between Wigan and Saints. Our major concern after our lack-lustre display against Barrow in the previous round was to guard against over confidence and to make sure that we did a thoroughly professional job and that was stressed throughout the week during training.

On the Tuesday evening one of the main events of David Creasser's testimonial year, the Radio Leeds *League Express Road Show*, was hosted

119

at the Meanwood Working Men's Club. I paid tribute to him in what was a very hard and emotional speech, especially as we have been close friends from school since the age of seven and had been through a lot together. His premature retirement through injury at the age of only twenty-seven was extremely sad and he would be the first to admit that, despite over a thousand points for Leeds and four caps for Great Britain, he did not have the chance to fulfil his true potential as a professional. It was heartening to see the number of old players supporting the event and most enjoyable for myself, David and Colin Maskill to beat legends Alan Smith, Syd Hynes and John Holmes in a light-hearted quiz. We often bump into a number of the ex-players such as Roy Dickinson, Kevin Dick and John Atkinson after matches and enjoy a good rapport and banter with them socially. They all like to pass comment on the games and catch up with club gossip and this occasion was no exception and enjoyed by all. The supporters' reception for me and towards certain questions directed at Doug especially regarding the captaincy situation was certainly appreciated, although he did respond very well to the enquiry and the night as whole proved to be an entertaining success, having attracted about five hundred people.

The late withdrawal of Kevin Iro from the side to face the Hornets meant a début for sixteen year old Paul Cook on the wing which made me feel quite old, particularly as he mentioned to me that he used to watch me from the terraces of the Boulevard as an eight year old. He was told that he would be playing on the Friday and trained with the squad and seemed very relaxed and confident at the prospect.

Rochdale (Home) - Silk Cut Challenge Cup 14/2/93

The weather reverted more towards a typical winter's scene, with drifting fog and strong winds and Rochdale took advantage to settle quite quickly and made it clear that they were not going to become fodder for us. They tried to mix it and upset us early on and nerves obviously got to "Cookie" as he knocked on the first time he saw the ball. Alan Tait, myself and Ellery as some of the senior pros told him to forget about it and we soon dropped into our rhythm, began to play some attractive football despite the conditions and never looked back. After the first score the floodgates seemed to open and we were determined to stick to our plan of not relenting and entertaining the crowd. We controlled the ball well and began to force Rochdale into mistakes which we capitalised on. Their response was to become a little bit hot headed and a couple of high tackles resulted in some isolated fracas as they tried to stem the flow. On this occasion it backfired for them as, if anything, it concentrated our minds on the job and made us more determined to keep up the pace and to play to our strengths. There were constant appeals to the referee and a fair amount of chatter between the players. I got embroiled with their centre, Matt Calland, who had already had a couple of shots at our players before he went at James Lowes for no reason. I reminded him that if he wanted to have a go at anyone then he should pick on someone his own size, like me for instance, or take the ball in and see how he liked it, but it was all something or nothing. With my experience I should have known better and we soon reverted to the best form of retribution, rattling up points. The finishing was quite lethal as we capitalised on every opening with good, incisive, unselfish support play that enabled us to execute our planned moves. Although we were annoyed at not keeping a clean sheet, we maintained the onslaught in a pleasing performance that matched the club's best ever score in a cup tie. Our dominance was such that I even had time to chat to the crowd about my diminishing goal kicking prowess having shouted across to Dougie that I would have a go if Simon Irving wanted a rest. That was followed by the personal satisfaction of a hat-trick of tries in about fifteen minutes, my first for Leeds since November 1989, which restored my reputation as a poacher. Rochdale had effectively given up by then as we completed our

121

comprehensive thirteen try rout to send the supporters home happy having given them value for money. No doubt their thoughts were on Wembley but the players were realistic enough to know that there would be a lot of great teams left in the third round, that they would pose an entirely different threat and that we would need to work even harder if we were to progress.

After the match there was the usual obligation to mix with the cup and match sponsors which is a vital duty for the players. Without sponsors' generous support, the code and sport in general would not survive and they deserve our thanks on the day. They are almost always knowledgeable and keen to discuss the game constructively and the lure of a couple of free drinks and a chance to relax and unwind for twenty minutes or so before joining the clamour of the family is always welcome. It is amazing how often your own kids want to kick you around when you've just come off the park even after having suffered it for real during the previous eighty minutes.

Chapter Twelve

Make or Break

Monday evening's cup draw was again favourable, pairing us against old rivals Castleford again at Headingley. The standard of the opposition was intensifying with each round and the added constant of home fixtures meant that we had the ideal criteria for a good run. It was always going to be a mouth-watering tie and the obvious choice for the BBC's televised game, giving us an opportunity to show the general Rugby League public how much we had progressed from the start of the season. Any psychological advantage which we may have had from our resounding Boxing Day League win was already forgotten and counted for nothing, even if at the time it had seemed to affect Castleford's confidence. We all knew how different one-off cup ties were and that there would not be a forty point margin this time. Immediately after the draw I attended a Sportsman's Dinner to raise funds for the club at which all our sponsors were present. It proved to be a great night to relax and reflect as well as wear a more formal attire than is usually associated with rugby players, which made a pleasant change.

Yet again Leeds had a blank weekend, the irony being that for once the entire squad was fully fit, on a roll and raring to go. The gap meant a few important days off to get away from the mounting pressures and Wembley talk that was starting to build around the club. We tried to steer clear of the growing publicity in an effort to maintain our low profile approach whilst individually concentrating on what would be required to progress. That determined attitude was taken into training that week by everyone. In the build up to the game I was on the panel for a question and answer session at Warrington which was a tremendous success. I went with Lee Crooks and Steve Molloy and Eddie Hemmings compèred a superb night that enabled us to meet and mingle with spectators from most of the Lancashire clubs. There were some excellent questions concerning Rugby League matters in general and the well organised evening was a most enjoyable diversion.

I went to Wilderspool as the Great Britain Captain having been reappointed when the initial squad was announced for the impending international in France. There were no surprise selections or omissions, the inclusion of form players like Andy Currier on his recall and Steve McNamara came as no real surprise. I had thought that Malcolm might have been tempted to use the two fixtures which were the only Tests of the season to blood some more new talent against a French side that was reputed to be not very strong and in preparation for the autumn visit here of the Kiwis. It is a popular misconception that trips to France make an exotic change for the players, most do not look forward to it as we struggle with the language, the attitude of the natives and the food. It is not a place I would choose to go even for an all-expenses-paid romantic weekend without the wife! It is more akin to a smash and grab raid, get in, do the job and get out as quickly as possible. The first hint of a possible conflict of interest then arose when the Rugby League hierarchy announced a series of mid-week league fixtures including our rearranged home game with Wigan which were to be played immediately prior to the departure for France. Whereas normally those selected for the international would have been exempted, on this occasion we were all permitted to play. In total that threatened to involve sixteen out of the original nineteen man squad and seemed to be asking for trouble. Malcolm had to postpone all his carefully planned training sessions knowing how vital the matches were for all the players concerned, including those of Saint Helens and Castleford who were also due to meet each other on the same evening. Quite farcically the Test was undoubtedly devalued as a consequence. There are few enough international fixtures available and they have to be treated with respect and prepared for properly, irrespective of the opponents if they are to remain of any use. Not only is it making unrealistic demands on the players to expect them to perform in three immensely hard games in the space of a week but it was not fair on the coach. At the time it was stressed that the decision was a one-off and would not happen again but the Wigan fixture had already been provisionally agreed for later in April when it was not anticipated that there would have been a backlog. That date would have suited spectators and sponsors far better than giving them merely seven days notice for what should have been the biggest home match of the season at Headingley.

I could not understand the reasoning behind this rapid rearrangement but all of a sudden we were involved in a crucial week that threatened to make or break the entire season and test our resolve to its limits. The comments of Castleford chairman David Poulter that our forwards were a weak link provided further incentive and determination if it were needed. His remarks and criticisms were cut out of the papers and displayed on the dressing-room wall in order to motivate our pack to prove him wrong. With a full strength squad available we named our side early in the week to maximize our preparations. Castleford decided to release the news of the impending departure back to Queensland of their coach Darryl Van de Velde at the end of the season in an attempt to spur their lads to even greater efforts for him. We were not particularly worried by the battle cry coming from Wheldon Road, the news was no real surprise within the game and it was more a case of the timing of the announcement carrying the greatest impact. In many ways the contest was personified by the friendly rivalry between myself and Lee Crooks and we were in great

---

demand for pictures and comments by the media, not least the *Yorkshire Evening Post*, who invited us through our clubs for tea together at the Holiday Inn in Leeds. A few people commented that we had obviously discreetly hidden the pint pots but we had a good laugh and a non too serious discussion about the likely outcome. We both knew that friendships would be suspended during the hostilities especially if we could get close enough to confront each other on the pitch. The one thing that this Leeds side seemed to have in contrast to others of recent years was the experience of people like Andy Gregory and Ellery who knew exactly what was required in pressurised do-or-die cup tie football and throughout the week's build up their calming influence and advice was a critical factor.

Castleford (Home) - Silk Cup Challenge Cup 27/2/93

Even arriving at Headingley an hour and three quarters before the kick off you could sense the electric atmosphere and nervous energy about the place which was already starting to fill up with spectators. By the time we came out for the warm up the ground was alive with expectation and anticipation. A minute's silence before the kick-off in honour of Bobby Moore allowed us time to compose and focus ourselves before the battle, although I was very disappointed to hear some idiots chanting and not observing the occasion with the proper decorum. Despite coming from a different arena, he epitomised all the best qualities associated with a true sportsman and was the finest ambassador for his country and his memory deserved the utmost respect.

The importance of the game was illustrated by the fact that for the first and only time our fitness co-ordinator, Dean Riddle, was wired up with headphones, presumably to enable instructions from Dougie to reach the players on the pitch whilst he was tending to them. I cannot say that I noticed any great difference except for the fact that he looked an even worse sight than usual. The opening exchanges were understandably ferocious with defences on top and despite some disputed decisions both lines remained intact. Alan Tait thought that he had scored early on and once Castleford had established some territorial ascendancy St. John Ellis had two good attempts in the corner including a disallowed try that was being debated long after the final whistle. I was the closest player to him as I tried to bundle him into touch as he went over and in all fairness I think that it was a legitimate score as he got the ball down before hitting the corner flag. We got the luck of the touch judge's decision and kicked on from that, whereas Cas seemed to allow it to play on their minds and we took advantage to get the vital first score with a penalty.

The long kicking game from both sides was effective and the play developed into a form of stalemate in the middle of the park as neither side wanted to make a mistake. When we did manage to burst their defensive line, Jim Fallon's superbly taken try in the corner which showed his great strength was a huge fillip for the side and justified not only the club's outlay on him but all our constant jibing with him at training where he is such a laid back character. The play the balls were quick, there was no holding down in the tackle and the game was played at a cracking pace as each side strove to control the possession. Overall Castleford had the advantage in the first half but we were still annoyed to concede a try right on the stroke of half-time to level things up. The most important part of any close game is the five minutes before and after the break when concentration has to be at its sharpest. Our lapse cost us and was unprofessional as we knew exactly how close we were to the interval hooter. To have gone in with the lead would have given us extra confidence, as it was Doug had to stress that Castleford had been more enthusiastic during the first forty minutes than we had and now they would have the advantage of the elements. His pep talk reaffirmed that the side that won would be the one that wanted it more and our second half display confirmed our renewed enthusiasm.

127

A first half injury to Peter Coyne meant that I was facing Graham Steadman in the second period. He is far more of an individualistic player who loves to take his opposite number on and has a lovely side step and a great turn of pace if you give him half a yard. I had to make sure that I was on top of him as quickly as possible. The uncompromising man-on-man tackling from both sides meant that the ball rarely found its way into the hands of the centres and the heat of the challenges dispelled the chill of a quick snow storm. Castleford had learnt the lessons of their Boxing Day trouncing and Tawera Nikau stood wider out to nullify my options and room which he did very well. The game was always going to go down to the wire and demanded patience, but the one time we did open out Jim Fallon again crashed through his opposite number to claim the decisive score. Simon Irving's superb touchline conversion to give us a six point lead was an immense relief and we decided to work the position for a clinching drop goal. To their credit Castleford responded with an immediate counter attack culminating in a successful penalty for an alleged spear tackle on Lee Crooks. The decision against Gary Mercer and myself seemed harsh, it is hard enough to get hold of the big fellow never mind turn him over.

In the remaining five or ten minutes we were put under tremendous pressure as Cas carved out three or four openings but our nerve held firm despite knowing the class of players we were up against. The team effort and commitment showed a different side of Leeds following on from the flamboyance of the earlier rounds. Much like our performance against Hull Kingston Rovers we had passed an important test of character when the chips were really down and won a match that in previous years or earlier that season we would have undoubtedly lost. We had a few drinks afterwards to celebrate although it was a shame that the Castleford lads went straight off from the dressing room and did not join us in the bar, no matter how disappointed they may have been at the outcome.

Getting to grips with 'Crooksie'. *(Credit - Andy Howard)*

The Castleford confrontation took a lot out of us physically, having only had one really competitive match in the preceding month. All the lads were carrying bumps and bruises at training on the Tuesday but we had really needed the work-out, especially as the biggest test of all, Wigan, loomed on the horizon. Our improvement from Christmas had been steady but confronting the Central Park outfit would be the measure of just how far we had come and put our progress into perspective. Wigan are a totally different team to play against than any other and with the pressure game they operate and continual strong defence they maintain it is very difficult to come up with a successful strategy to outwit them. We decided that the most effective way would be to fight fire with fire and to try to beat them at their own tactics by insuring numbers in the tackles in an effort to slow them down and prevent them from dictating matters. A long and accurate kicking game would be essential, backed up by a totally committed chase which would hopefully pressure them into unforced mistakes.

Of immediate concern was the semi-final draw and I had no real preference for either the first or second date as we did not have a fixture pile up to worry about. With neutral venues, our only hope was to avoid Wigan. I was in the *Look North* studio as the draw was made on the Monday evening so that I could pass comment and prior to going live there were two rehearsals. In the first one we drew Oldham or Bradford and in the second we got Wigan so it was no real surprise that when it really mattered the third time round we were paired with the winners of the Hull Kingston Rovers and Widnes replay. I was happy with the outcome although a meeting with Bradford would have been nice as it would have guaranteed a Yorkshire side in the Wembley final.

For once there were no real favourites going into the Wigan match, they lacked a couple of regulars and we had remained unbeaten for over two months and were on home soil where we had not lost since the opening day of the season. Despite the fact that the game had been arranged with almost indecent haste, it represented an excellent opportunity to really put Leeds back on the Rugby League map. I was pleased to have been named the Club Player of the Month for February by our sponsors, Hammond Suddards, which was a reward for consistency rather than based on a single performance, but that guaranteed nothing for the future. Our large ex-Wigan contingent, especially Andy Gregory and Kevin Iro who were facing them for the first time, gave us a greater insight into their methods, motivations and style of football and we felt ready for them.

Wigan (Home) - Stones Bitter Championship 3/3/93

There is something unique about the atmosphere at a night match, particularly when the ground is almost full and it inevitably transfers itself to the players. The enormous twenty thousand gate caused a delay to the kick-off as they packed on to the terraces which was annoying as we were itching to get out there having already finished applying our vaseline and resin when the touch judge came in to inform us. The priority must always be crowd safety and the only solution is to remain quiet and calm, clearly visualising your required role on the pitch. Once we had been greeted by the cacophony of sound and noise and finally got down to business, the speed of both defences off the mark was incredible and, as we had planned, forced Wigan into some uncharacteristic mistakes as we started to put them off their stride. The overall pace of the play gave no one any time to think although we did manage to carve out an early opening for Jim Fallon but he unfortunately lost the ball as he attempted to touch down. Both defences remained on top and impervious to the direct running of the forwards and with the level of experience on show every known professional trick was on display, most notably at the play the ball in attempt to gain an advantage. There was a lot of talk to match officials from players on both sides but the referee held firm and was not frightened of making decisions.

Soon after Jim's miss I allowed myself to be distracted as I tried to switch play and Martin Dermott came up quickly and picked off the pass to scamper about forty yards to the line, a distance I had never seen him go before. After our confident opening, it was important for our forwards to reassert themselves and impose their presence as they continued their war of attrition in an attempt to secure the backs a good position from which to launch a counter. A brawl seemed inevitable at some stage as the tensions increased. When it erupted it was more a case of shadow boxing, there being more numbers than fists, but it led to the sin-binning of Steve Molloy and Neil Cowie, two Oldham lads who obviously have a fierce rivalry. In their absence we kept plugging away, knowing that there was very little between the sides, and were rewarded by a well worked try between the posts from Alan Tait after a speciality half dummy from Andy Gregory. The crowd were ecstatic and really got behind us as we approached half-time deservedly level. Yet again, though, we succumbed to our new fault of conceding a score at a crucial stage, just as the hooter was about to sound, although this time the try by Andrew Farrar was hotly disputed and appeared to be a double movement.

We were a little unlucky to be behind at the break and felt that we were in with a real chance of victory if we could start dictating play for a period of time. We knew that their defence was not invincible and that, if we could break the stranglehold that Wigan always put on their opponents by denying them room, we could create the necessary chances to score points. Unfortunately, Wigan's opening to the second half was their usual prodigious effort and they controlled that critical period when they are normally at their most dangerous and effective. They were helped by our mistakes in possession that enabled them to gain a territorial foothold which eventually led to Martin Offiah streaking over in the corner, which was a real blow as we felt that they were not two scores better than us at that stage. In some respects, the referee was too far away from the play the ball area as he endeavoured to try and keep the sides apart which led to some niggling but he was not helped in that respect by his touch judges.

Our heads dropped a little and Wigan sensed victory and, like the ultra professional side that they are, moved in for the kill, especially as our frustration and panic played right into their hands. They took control and effectively cut off our route of supply to the centres and wingers. Injuries to key players and necessary reshuffles did not help our cause but there was a remorseless inevitability about Wigan's performance.

Afterwards, we contemplated on the gap that still existed between ourselves and the very best and that we needed to concentrate harder and for longer. Wigan's dominance is based partly on their immense playing strength but also on an almost unshakeable belief in their ability, bred by a fierce will and the enjoyment of winning. They never seem to get complacent about or tired of success and are mentally and physically tough enough to respond in the big games and pressure situations. The experience they have gained brings the best out of them when it really matters. We had surrendered our winning run but were not too despondent, knowing that we had not suddenly become a bad side overnight and that the margin of defeat did not really reflect the game and flattered Wigan. The lessons had to be learnt and the continuing hard work ahead was obvious as the ultimate test of a good side is how they respond to a setback. That is also where the best coaches earn their money when picking their players up from the disappointment of defeat.

After the match, the internationals in the two sides suddenly became team mates and by midnight we had rung Malcolm Reilly at his home to let him know whether we would be available to report for training the next day in preparation for the excursion to France. By then our semi-final opponents and venue were known and there was the chance of revenge for our Regal Trophy Final defeat the season before with a repeat clash against Widnes at Central Park. People were starting to talk about the possibility of a "dream final" between the game's heavyweights of ourselves and Wigan but we knew that being our first Challenge Cup semi-final since 1986 we could not afford to take anything for granted.

133

The Great Britain squad met at Headingley for fitness testing the next morning to assess the carnage of the midweek fixtures. Seven players had been forced to withdraw and there were only six fit enough to train which led to Malcolm cancelling the session as he hurriedly sought replacements. The late inclusion of some of the younger players who Malcolm may have been thinking of drafting in for the return home tie did not really affect the team's spirit as we knew that they would not let anybody down and were ready for the step up to international football. The two match series against France was our only real preparation for the Kiwis and it was vital to maintain our ongoing efforts to match and beat the best from the southern hemisphere. The decision to take the First Test against the New Zealanders to Wembley had already been taken and if we wanted to attract the necessary crowd and support, it was imperative that we prepared thoroughly for the French. The revised party met for the first time at Manchester Airport on the Friday morning at quarter to nine for the 10.30 flight to Toulouse where we made our base, some hour and a half from the match venue of Carcassonne. Soon after we had arrived and claimed our hotel rooms Malcolm called the first team meeting. Advance warnings of snow and therefore limited facilities proved to be unfounded as the weather was very pleasant for training. By necessity, the session was light and lethargic as most of the players were still feeling the effects of the midweek matches and were tired from the travelling, having been up early in the morning.

The standard of our accommodation was good, although the same could not be said of the food. As well as taking some of our own, there was fortunately a McDonalds right across the road from the hotel and along with the under-nineteen Academy lads who were with us, we spent a fair amount of time in there boosting their profits. The majority of players who had won late call ups were from Widnes but at no time was there any talk of the semi or attempts by the various protagonists to 'psyche' each other out. Malcolm would not have wanted nor expected talk of domestic football when in the international arena and concentrating on Test match requirements, and this was carried on into the social side. Because of the club versus country conflict which had been shown to have terribly backfired, we were left with just one forty-five minute training session to integrate the side. We had worked out a simple game plan at our Friday night meeting and aimed to capitalise on the experience of the nucleus of the side. The French media were conspicuous by their absence which may have been an indication of how the code was struggling over there. We had heard that they did not have a particularly strong side in spite of containing a couple of Aussies who had apparently qualified by residential right. I cannot see how that can be good for the development of the game as a whole and it could well become the thin end of the wedge regarding international representation and should not be allowed to happen. The decision to make the Academy Test into a double header rather than play it to a few hundred spectators the day before as previously was, however, an enterprising move and provided them with the added benefit of being around the senior players. We did not mix at training or meal times but chatted with them in the hotel whenever we met. They were certainly a massive bunch and I was glad that I was not playing at that level because they were far too big for me.

France v Great Britain - British Coal Test 7/3/93

On the journey to the stadium I could not picture whether I had played at Carcassonne before but when I arrived I recognised the dome shaped venue as the one where Mike Gregory had suffered his nose and cheek bone being broken in two places in an unsavoury match in the late eighties.

The facilities were very basic and outmoded and the pitch rock hard and surrounded by a banked cycling track. A very strong wind was blowing into the arena and was caught in the bowl effect which meant that the kicking strategy would be paramount. Malcolm asked me beforehand if I was going to play with or against it but unfortunately the decision was taken out of my hands when I lost the toss and they decided to try and use it to their advantage. As we lined up for the anthems I noticed that the opposition were the smallest French side I had ever played against or seen and I stressed to our forwards that, despite any pre-match talk of how the French were likely to mix it and sort us out, if their stature was any indication then we really should have been able to dominate them. That is exactly what happened, after the initial big hits in the early stages, I got the first try which was important in settling the side down and establishing our plan. Even with a front row comprising three new caps, Neil Cowie, Steve McCurrie and Steve Molloy, our defensive organisation was spot-on right from the start and they were also going forward and setting the line up well. Malcolm's plan of holding the ball for as long as possible in the early stages and keeping the French pinned in their own twenty-five was very effective throughout the first half. The French were competitive during those first forty minutes but by the break we had built up an almost unassailable 18-6 lead against the elements and knew that we were in control.

Early in the second period we started lethargically and allowed them more yards than we should have done but a couple more tries seemed to knock the spirit out of them and we proceeded to score almost at will in the later stages to run up a record away victory as they lost heart. The French crowd do not tend to appreciate or applaud the efforts of the opposition and most of the noise in the ground came from the two hundred or so travelling fans who were given good cause to make their presence felt. We were extremely satisfied with our display, we had played some good rugby in spite of the ludicrous lack of preparation which had not been up to standard and made the job doubly difficult. The new lads emerged with credit and justified their late selections. I bagged another hat trick which was personally satisfying and allowed the media to focus on my nearing the records for both Great Britain appearances and tries. That was my fortieth Test and took my try tally to thirty, still some way behind Mick Sullivan's totals of forty-one tries in forty-six appearances. I like to think of myself as more of a creator than scorer these days and in fact I could have had five tries that afternoon but Ellery and Mike Ford were in support and better positioned. In the back of my mind is the thought that I would dearly like to be Britain's most capped player but I know that Malcolm will only pick his sides on the basis of form and not sentiment. It is still important to have goals to aspire for, though. I joked with the press corps afterwards that in view of the performance there was obviously nothing wrong with the preparation and that we would be looking to repeat it prior to the series with the Kiwis. The fact that we got away with it should not give licence for such situations ever to be allowed to happen again if Test match rugby is to be taken seriously as the pinnacle of the sport. The standard of the opposition is not our problem but the winning of Test caps should always remain meaningful and they should not be given away.

The after-match official reception at the Town Hall in Carcassonne lasted about half an hour and comprised of a few speeches from the respective hierarchies, the French ones being translated for us by Harry Jepson who can actually speak the language better than his English. We then journeyed back to the hotel in Toulouse for our own version put on by our sponsors, British Coal, which also included their guests. A lot of the squad were very tired and suffering the effects of a surfeit of matches. Your body can only take so much and with a major semi-final in the offing, rest and recovery were the priority, even allowing for the odd hangover the next morning.

Sheffield (Home) - Stones Bitter Championship 7/3/93

Leeds were involved in a vital match with the Eagles at the same time as our French encounter and we knew how important a victory was to the whole squad to restore confidence after the Wigan defeat and in preparation for the semi. Some more of the emerging young talent at Headingley was given its head and we were asking immediately after our match if any of the media lads knew the score. We had heard that Sheffield had taken the lead and that Leeds had hit back to gain a slender half-time advantage but when the final score came through of a resounding victory, spearheaded by seventeen year old stand-off Graham Holroyd on his début, we were delighted. In many ways that match and its eventual result mirrored what the Great Britain squad had been through, late withdrawals, a lack of available preparation and a glimpse of the next generation. The Leeds result avenged our dismal display at the Don Valley and proved that some of the youngsters waiting in the wings had been schooled in the right habits and are ready for first team action if needed as the squad depth increases. Their development under the Rugby League's Apprenticeship Scheme and with the influence of the senior professionals around the place should be assured and it is easy to see even in training that the lads have a touch of class about them. I have always been a firm believer in the adage that if you are good enough then you are old enough. Inevitably, comparisons were being made between Graham Holroyd and myself, especially as his second try came from an interception which people tend to regard as my trademark. I am sure that he does not want to be saddled with that early on in his career and he will be keen to make his own unique identity and mark.

Relief at having made it through to the semis. *(Credit - Andy Howard)*

Chapter Thirteen

Curse of the Chemics

The return journey from France was our last chance to relax genuinely before the intensity of the semi and the stocks of duty free on the plane were somewhat depleted. At training on the Tuesday morning Dougie asked us if we were all fit and the only problem was Kevin Iro who had hobbled off during the Sheffield clash with a recurrence of his hamstring pull. There was never really any realistic possibility of him being fit to face Widnes despite all talk of his treatment in an oxygen tank and having an outside possibility of making the side. The discussions in our team meeting centred on responding to the continuing criticism of our ageing forwards. The Widnes six, even without Paul Moriarty and Essene Faimalo, were being touted as a more formidable pack, especially by their coach Phil Larder, and he expected them to exploit our weaknesses. In contrast to the Regal Final against them we were making no predictions and hoping for a more reasoned analysis from the media this time around. I had mentioned to some of the reporters on the flight back from France that we preferred it that way and I was hoping that we would just be allowed to get on with the job.

Whilst we prepared for the most important club match of the season, the League decided to wash its dirty linen in public again by announcing a complete U-turn over the restructuring debate and the immediate imposition

141

of two divisions for the coming season, even though there were only five weeks of the current one left to run. The revised formula would mean the loss of three sides from the competition and not only did the declaration effectively rob this season of the majority of its interest and incentive but allowed the sport to become a laughing stock, particularly in the eyes of its detractors. Claims that we were a professional game run by amateurs appeared to have a ring of truth about them as the immorality of it flew in the face of natural justice. The implementation of a working party to study the feasibility of summer rugby only added insult to injury. From the opinion that I had canvassed throughout the game, the players were completely against it.

The Leeds side was announced on the Thursday and confirmed that Kevin Iro would be absent which was a blow that we had to quickly put behind us. The dilemma of who to play on the wing was solved by the recall of Vince Fawcett who was offered the chance to put his nightmare at Hull KR behind him whilst Graham Holroyd had impressed sufficiently in half a match to retain his place on the bench. There was never any question that I would not play because of an ear infection or that at the last minute I had wanted to withdraw and had been forced to turn out by Doug. I had suffered a slight reaction to the tendonitis behind my knee in training on the Friday night but the ear problem was a long-standing one dating back two years which had progressively become worse over the previous four or five months. What was initially a perforated ear drum had become infected and I saw the specialist on my return from France and he confirmed that it would be necessary to have a look at the extent of the damage under general anaesthetic but in view of the importance of this Widnes tie that was put off for a week. The fact that my hearing was deteriorating in my right ear did not affect my balance or my ability to perform on the pitch but was more of an embarrassment at home and socially.

The huge spur for Widnes coming into the semi-final was their ongoing financial crisis. This match represented their players' only real chance to secure their seasonal contract payments which had already been cut back. We knew that the Widnes lads were on more of a win bonus than we were but the motivation of going to Wembley far outweighed anything else.

Widnes (Central Park) - Silk Cut Challenge Cup 13/3/93

The mood on the coach to the game was pretty quiet. We met at the Lawnswood Arms rather than at Headingley in an effort to avoid the wellwishers who turn up to cheer you off before the big occasions as they had before the Regal Final. I thought that it was a strange decision as it is important to allow the fans that kind of involvement and a bit sad that we were leaving from a pub rather than more familiar surroundings. A lot was made about the duel between myself and Jonathan Davies as being one of the key areas and I knew all about his pace, side step and kicking ability despite criticisms about his lack of size. During his introduction to the code he was shuffled around the back line as he was brought on but he has adapted very well and his phenomenal scoring record is a testimony to his class. When we arrived at the ground we went out to inspect the pitch and measure the swirling cross wind which we would have liked to have played with if we had won the toss. Even at that time there were about three thousand Leeds fans around the place which was awash with blue and amber. By the time we came out for the warm up fifteen minutes before the kick-off the overall atmosphere was unbelievable. Both sides were forced to go through their routines behind the posts as a curtain raiser was still in progress. This brought us even closer to the spectators but we tried to remain calm and detached especially as a lot of our lads had not experienced anything like that before.

We were expecting to be bullied early on as we had been in the league

143

encounter at Headingley but this time it did not happen. Although the teams were keen to get to each other, we were not kept ten metres apart as the referee was policing the ruck which meant that it was even more difficult to make the yards. We had managed to settle quite well and did not look vulnerable on defence and so were disappointed with the manner in which we conceded the first try after ten minutes. Bobby Goulding's kick across the face of the posts into the corner caught us unawares and although he seemed to be up there very quickly, David Myers did well to catch it on the full to score. It was undoubtedly a planned move which took us by surprise and as we regrouped behind the posts we were determined to put that behind us and fully expected Jonathan Davies to miss the conversion from wide out. When it sailed over it must have given Widnes an even bigger boost as it was a real sickener for us. We needed a quick response and a couple of half breaks gave us the position for a successful penalty to reduce the deficit although the decision by the referee not to put anyone in the sin bin for a professional foul was a little mystifying. Immediately after the restart there was further controversy as to whether Widnes had put the ball out on the full, which would have been a penalty to us on halfway, or if the ball had bounced in field before going out, which would have resulted with us dropping out from between the posts and handing them back possession in a threatening position. Gary Mercer positioned himself on the dead ball line and his decision to leave the kick was vindicated when the touch judge initially signalled ball back before changing his mind. We were immediately put back under pressure and Bobby Goulding turned it into points with a drop goal on the last tackle. Widnes had their tails up and made two or three clean breaks and although our defence was desperate at times, most notably when the wingers came back to make try-saving tackles, it was effective. Everyone in the Leeds side was working for each other and we were trying to spread the load on both attack and defence in order to pace ourselves and get everyone involved in the game. In an effort to obtain the best field position players were tending to scoot from acting half-back which, although it denied the backs the ball, helped us to weather the early Widnes storm. We were constantly saying to each other throughout the first half that they seemed to be tiring and towards the end of it we were starting to dictate matters even though we were behind.

Going to the break at only 7-4 down we were not disheartened and everyone was as confident and enthusiastic as when we had first gone out. In the dressing-room we thought that if we could contain them for the first fifteen or twenty minutes of the second period that we could go on and win it, especially as we had the advantage of the wind and felt that their bigger forwards, Kurt Sorensen and Emosi Koloto, were starting to struggle. Tragically for us, the breakthrough at the start of the half came their way courtesy of one of our mistakes when Alan Tait could not hold a high bomb and John Devereux crashed over for a lucky try in the corner. If we were deflated by that, then Jonathan Davies' second superb conversion really hurt us, although even at 13-4 behind we felt we could go on with the job. From then on, though, things went from bad to worse and as we tried to force the ball playing catch up we let the game plan slip. The pack stopped going forward, the half-backs were doing nothing, no openings were created and the centres and wingers might as well have been in the stand for the number of times we lost the ball on the first tackle. I let Andy Currier get outside me and missed the tackle close to the line and at 17-4 we knew the game had gone from us. It is almost impossible to lift players behind the posts when they know they are not going to Wembley no matter how experienced they are. The weight of disillusion is enormous, particularly for letting down the fans and despite what was said afterwards our only incentive was personal pride and the hope of sticking in there and closing the gap. Perhaps inevitably, the harder we tried the more unforced errors we made, and Widnes were on such a high that they gratefully accepted them to inflate the winning margin and turn the second half into a rout. We could not use the excuse of carrying injuries in key positions, we were all

145

fully fit when we took the field but criticism of the older, more senior professionals for their lack of leadership and not setting the right example was unfair. All the players did try to give a hundred per cent commitment and did not intentionally go out to play badly but perhaps suffered from human frailties. Unfortunately for the club and its fans that seems to happen on the bigger occasions and it is certainly true that a semi-final is the worst place to lose.

The dissection of our late capitulation took away a lot of credit from the Widnes performance, especially by those players who had been on the transfer list or in dispute with the club such as Darren Wright, Andy Currier, David Myers and Jonathan Davies. The way that they stuck together and rallied round in adversity to try and secure their future must have given them great cause for satisfaction and built a great spirit and bonding within the club. I was not given any explanation as to why I was substituted for the last five minutes. I was not injured and, although I would be the first to admit that I did not play well, there were plenty of other players who were under-achieving. Maybe it was just to give Graham Holroyd a run in his favourite position or perhaps it was more a gesture of giving the public a scapegoat. That action certainly added fuel to the later innuendo and renewed speculation about my future. The feeling of total dejection at the final whistle was almost impossible to put into words and the thought of the Widnes side walking out at Wembley instead of us was practically unbearable. We also knew that there was no way that they were over thirty points better than us and that we had failed to justify our personal reputations. There was only total silence in the dressing-room afterwards, no explanations or recriminations, just a collective realisation that we had let ourselves, our families, the club, the city and our loyal supporters down. Any thoughts that the Leeds players were not bothered or affected by the outcome because of their lucrative contracts was way off the mark. Like all clubs in the recession, there was talk of Leeds having to make contract cutbacks for the next season and eight of the squad had theirs up for renewal. The loss of extraneous income through souvenirs, sponsorship and future season ticket sales was incalculable amongst the wreckage of the defeat. It was undoubtedly a time for review and introspection on the playing side and gave the coaching staff food for thought regarding rebuilding and boosting morale for the final leg of the league programme leading to the end of season Premiership competition. The margin of our defeat left us wide open to the old accusations about divisions within the club and personality clashes off the field which surfaced on the terraces and in the media and which was inevitable and complete nonsense. A witch hunt was the last thing the club needed and the only real excuse was that collectively we did not perform to anything like our true capabilities on the day. What does stick are the taunts such as big-spending Leeds flatter to deceive, but as I have said, facts do not tell lies, and until we win something we have to take the flak associated with playing for the biggest club in the game. There seemed little doubt that the club would have to dip again into the transfer market and to keep strengthening until the side was good enough to win things. The longer a run of losses goes on in big games, the harder it is to shed the tag of "nearly men" and avoid freezing on such occasions.

As the reality dawned the next morning, I read the reviews in the Sunday papers but they did not tell me anything new. In the evening I attended Trevor Skerret's fortieth birthday party along with old friends Graham Idle, David Topliss and a lot of people from the Bison's Amateur Club as well as quite a few Leeds supporters. Although the semi-final result cast a shadow it in no way spoilt a most enjoyable evening. As far as I knew, the club planned no crisis meetings or inquests and so it came as something of a surprise when on the Monday evening as the family was having tea at Colin Maskill's, to hear his brother Roy say that I was in trouble again. He informed me that *Look North* had carried a report by Harry Gration claiming that there would be a big board meeting at Headingley the next

147

day at which I was going to be transfer listed and Doug Laughton's future was up for discussion and on the line. When I returned home I rang my dad and asked him if there had been any official comment from the club but he told me that they had not sought any in the report and so I dismissed it as journalistic licence for the sake of jumping on the bandwagon. At the only team meeting we did have earlier that day, Dougie had stressed the need to look forward rather than back and prepare for the league encounter again against Widnes in that midweek in the right frame of mind.

I was out of contention for that rearranged game and the rest of the week's training as a result of my exploratory ear operation. The prognosis was that I needed a major operation which I delayed to the end of the season as it would have meant two months out of the game. The boys headed off to Widnes with a mix-and-match side showing several players out of position and an all ex-Rugby Union back line for the worst possible fixture that they could have been handed and one which would be the ultimate test of their nerve.

Widnes (Away) - Stones Bitter Championship 17/3/93

I listened to the game on the radio at home as I convalesced after the anaesthetic and it sounded as though the side had responded with a lot of spirit and heart and battled through a match in which they were heavily penalised. Naughton Park is not the sort of venue I normally relish going to, for despite the dressing-rooms being good, the pitch is untidy and with due respect to their supporters it is not a place to take the family. We never thought it likely that the match would be littered with vendettas from the semi or previous encounters, it was more a matter of regaining lost pride for the club and restoring faith for the fans. Much was made of the launch of the "Widnes in Need" appeal by Jim Mills before and during the game and it is hard to ignore the plight of friends in trouble although I doubt that any of the Leeds players or supporters signed up for the lottery.

Steve Pilgrim became the twenty-ninth player used by the club during the season which might have explained some of our lack of consistency for, whilst a big squad is essential, the ideal number of regular players should be around twenty-two. Again it appeared that we put ourselves under pressure with early mistakes that were punished but we responded with a greater resolve. I am not a particularly good listener at the best of times and the coverage was in conjunction with Bradford's league clash with Wigan at Odsal which they went on to win and the inevitable comparisons between our performance and that of our greatest rivals were made which I did not enjoy hearing. The impression gained was that we had fought hard in defeat and had not been intimidated by their attempts at provocation. We seemed to have channelled our aggression into effectively disrupting their play and even though that occasionally manifested itself in indiscipline, the general consensus was that we were unlucky to lose.

The special mail bag in the following night's *Yorkshire Evening Post* that was supposed to explain our semi-final performance produced the usual simplistic and biased explanations that were not really worthy of note. I am sure the fans' frustrations and hurt were as deep as that of the players and if I had been part of the management or directors of the club I would have held an open meeting at Headingley with the coach, captain and a few of the players for the supporters to air their grievances and get straight and honest answers in return, rather than leave them to just write in and make the sort of scathing comments that they would not dare in a face-to-face situation. The week as a whole had been one of the most difficult in my professional career and I did not intend to accept being held solely responsible for what had been a collective failure.

The team returned to Headingley to host Wakefield very much on trial

149

after the successive setbacks against the Chemics. Prior to the kick off I went into the dressing-room and the lads were obviously apprehensive about the likely size of the crowd and what their reaction would be. They knew that they would have to generate their own atmosphere and to work hard to earn the fans' full support. If they did not know what to expect, then I was also in for a surprise. The match marked my first appearance at the club that week after my exploratory operation and at around twenty to three Doug Laughton called me into his office, locked the door behind me, and informed me that he had decided to suspend me for two weeks for breaching the club rules on reporting in when injured and thereby missing training. He told me that I would receive a letter of confirmation in the post the next day and that I would not be required to attend the club for any reason during that period. His justification was that I had not gone through the correct channels by failing to consult with the club physio and doctor in the first instance although both had known for about four or five months that I had been suffering with my hearing and that I had arranged to see a specialist on my return from France. As far as I was concerned, the condition was deteriorating and needed some immediate attention, at least to the extent of ascertaining the level of the damage. In retrospect I realised that I had not approached the matter in the right manner and had gone ahead and made my own arrangements motivated solely by my primary and only concern of looking after my long term health. I had genuinely felt that it was something that I had to do and I explained the aim behind my actions but a long discussion was clearly not required and I knew that I had to face up to his decision however much it hurt.

Wakefield (Home) - Stones Bitter Championship 21/3/93

Stunned by the news, I retreated to the private box of the sponsors of my car, N.I.C., to watch the game from behind glass whilst the impact began to sink in. I had been in dispute with my previous side, Hull, over a legitimate contractual argument but club suspensions were comparatively rare within the game and the only other player I could think of who had been in a similar position was my mate, Bobby Goulding. The implications certainly distressed me very deeply.

In common with a lot of other Yorkshire clubs, Wakefield love nothing more than to turn Leeds over and if possible embarrass them at Headingley. Their intense rivalry which may be rooted in an envy of our profile and facilities always ensures that they raise their game one hundred and twenty per cent no matter what the occasion. Even if this fixture had lost some of its significance with the decision to scrap relegation, relieving Trinity of any lingering worries, we were sure that their players had every incentive to get a result. Ellery continued at stand-off which meant that in effect we were playing with an extra supporting forward in the backs rather than a genuine play maker.

Andy Gregory was still there to call the moves and we began very well putting on some set ploys and making good yardage which was rewarded with some early points. We dominated the opening quarter to take a 14-0 lead which was vital for winning back the sceptics amongst the fans and got them firmly on our side. Having missed the reverse fixture at Belle Vue because of the World Cup Final I would have liked to have opposed Nigel Wright, Trinity's teenage sensation who was one of the finds of the season. He is surely destined to be a future Great Britain stand-off although hopefully not for a while yet. He has great balance, vision and an ability to bring his backs into play and is one of the most promising of a large crop of young talent currently in the game.

Despite such a positive start, which also included some good cover defence near our own line, we contrived to squander our advantage. We lacked a killer punch and allowed Wakefield back into the game with two tries prior to half-time to cut the deficit. To their credit they battled away with some enterprising rugby and really came out firing after the interval. Again we made it easy for them by dropping our concentration and enthusiasm and forgetting the basics rather than sticking to a winning plan. Our growing frustration and almost resignation handed them the initiative and in a mirror image of the first half they overwhelmed us in the initial quarter of the second period to score fourteen unanswered points. Our need to play desperation football was bound to induce mistakes in our play and fortunately Trinity bombed a certain try in the corner with a three man overlap. That signalled the Leeds lads to rally round and they hauled themselves back into the game to ensure an exciting finish. The introduction of our two young substitutes, Paul Anderson and Graham Holroyd, seemed to help especially as "Holly's" kicking game gave us more variation and helped pin Wakefield back in their own half. His half-back combination with James Lowes, who reverted to his original role at Hunslet of scrum half, was not ideal as neither of them had played together before but was effective in getting the ball wider and faster to the centres. All the team responded to the fresh impetus and heart and they staged a valiant comeback which culminated in Simon Irving scoring a last gasp try in the corner to level the scores. His attempted conversion with the final kick of the match just drifted wide and we had done it tough to salvage a draw and some respectability.

The crowd seemed to enjoy the open game if not the final outcome and had come alive towards the end of the encounter even though there had been an element of late season fare about some of the play. It had been a warm afternoon and on occasions the defences had resembled a game of touch and pass which again proved to me to be a convincing argument against summer rugby. Any home draw is always a point lost rather than gained but I imagined that the mood in the dressing-room afterwards was one of relief. In contrast, I sought out our Commercial Manager to inform

152

him of my suspension which, amongst other things, meant that a planned midweek meeting of the Blue and Amber Club featuring a question and answer session with myself and Lee Crooks could not go ahead. I went into the players' bar to collect my wife and son and headed home to await the inevitable reaction.

Chapter Fourteen

The Eye of a Storm

The news broke with glaring headlines in the press and on the radio throughout the following day. Not surprisingly it was made into a clash of personalities between myself and Doug who had stated publicly that the decision was solely his and gave cause for the journalists to rake over the coals of the season starting with the Manly affair and focusing on some of both mine and the team's poorer performances. I did not think that it was intended to be anything other than a salutary lesson and a reminder to everyone at the club that a disciplinary code has to be adhered to and that no one could be allowed to step out of line. He stressed the need for the senior players to set the correct example for the up and coming youngsters but in my defence I honestly believed that I had not intentionally done anything wrong. Even if I did feel that the punishment was a little harsh, I knew that I had to accept it and the accompanying consequences. One of those was that being the Great Britain captain the story gained a national prominence. I hoped that once the circumstances were known and it was accepted that there was not an actual conflict, my reputation would remain intact. Of greater concern was the realisation that if some of the fans had accepted that I was the semi-final scapegoat then this was the equivalent of offering me as a ritual sacrifice although I was sure that that had not been Doug's intention. All the spectators would have no doubt voiced their own opinions and loyalties; the whole episode was bound to have confirmed a few prejudices and that was understandable no matter how unjust or disparaging their perceptions were. All the players knew that if they missed training and did not inform the club or offer a reasonable or acceptable excuse they would be heavily fined but an actual suspension was very unusual.

The other major implication was that my hope of leading Great Britain in the return fixture against the French was in severe jeopardy, not only because the management rightly refused to pick players who were ineligible to play for their clubs, but also because the game was due to be played at Headingley and I had been banned from the ground. Being denied the opportunity to represent your country which is the highest honour in any sport, is bad enough but the fact that I was chasing and dearly wanted to set the record for most appearances made it worse. The chance for a couple more tries had also seemed likely in my dual quest for a place in the history books. As soon as I was able to I rang the Rugby League's Public Affairs Executive, David Howes, to inform him of the situation and stress that I was not actually in dispute with Leeds, rather that it was the other way round. He promised to speak to Maurice Lindsay, the Chief Executive, in an attempt to get clarification as to whether I could still play and promised to phone me back the next day. When Maurice did call on the Monday afternoon after the matter had been raised at a meeting of the Rugby League Board of Directors, it was to confirm my worst fears that there could be no exceptions to the ruling.

In spite of frequent requests from the media for my comments on the decision I maintained a diplomatic silence and tried to play the matter down. I did not think that there was any need to elaborate and that anything I did say would not stop people from drawing their own conclusions. There seemed little point in running the risk of aggravating the situation when I had already accepted the reasoning behind it. After the initial furore had died down, some calming statements did emerge from both sides. The club stressed that I had definitely not been put on the transfer list; I vowed to return to training at the earliest opportunity and asserted that I remained totally committed to Leeds. That, of course, did not stop various high profile pundits from offering their opinions, most notably in the columns of the *League Express* newspaper and by Mike Stephenson on *Boots 'n All*. Both of them reckoned that Leeds was not big enough for the two of us and that one or other or possibly even both of us were going to have to leave which was never the case. In any partnership, like a marriage, there are always differences and something would be wrong if there were not disagreements at some time. The most important thing was that we were both interested only in what was best for Leeds and putting the club back where it belonged. In that respect we were pulling in the same direction and were determined to at least fulfil if not extend our respective contracts.

It felt extremely strange not to get a letter from the Great Britain management on the Tuesday morning informing me of my selection and where to report for training and when I did see the squad in the paper I noticed with some surprise that Jonathan Davies had been named as my replacement. I had expected his team mate Bobby Goulding to get a recall with Shaun Edwards moving to cover the stand off berth. Jonathan is more of a support player than a creator but his inclusion was also important with regard to taking over the goal kicking role. Much as I would have loved to have been involved and participate in the Great Britain preparations at any level that was never a realistic possibility as the game's hierarchy could not be seen to be taking sides. I was in full agreement with the decision to make Andy Platt captain and he would have been my choice, even though I am sure that Philip Clarke will eventually take over. I was certain that Andy would handle the responsibility admirably and would lead by example in his usual way which would command the respect of the other players.

I managed to keep occupied during the first week of my suspension as it coincided with us moving house which tended to keep my mind off my predicament although it would definitely have been less stressful and physically demanding to have gone training. It was unfortunate that the format for the Blue and Amber meeting had to be changed at the last minute as I had been really looking forward to it and I was sure that the kids would have had some interesting questions prepared for Lee about his time and experiences at Leeds.

Hull (Home) - Stones Bitter Championship 28/3/93

Once again I had to resort to reports on the radio to follow Leeds' progress against my former club. Owing to the understandable lack of continuity of the coverage with so many other matches to follow, it was difficult to make sense of a game whose score fluctuated so frequently. What was obvious from the commentary was that both sides' commitment to open play was considerably eased by defensive lapses particularly round the play the ball area. I have never had mixed feelings about wanting the side to do well in my absence and if they could have won by fifty points then I would have been delighted.

The match was refereed by Aussie, Graham Annesly, as part of his preparations for the forthcoming Test and in general I think that their occasional presence is good for the British game and that their standard and interpretation of the laws should serve as a yard-stick for most of those officiating over here. They have a great rapport with the players and prefer to be unobtrusive and make sure that they stick to the task of letting the game flow.

We again managed to cruise into a big lead with some impressive support play before stepping off the gas and allowing Hull to close the gap before the interval. An ability to score spectacular tries could not mask an indisciplined defensive display which must have given both coaches nightmares as the play must have resembled an unopposed training session

The Eye of a Storm

however entertaining that may have appeared. The majority of spectators would probably have been happy at witnessing an average of a point a minute but the players would have known the limitations of their own performances. Such high scoring results are common at that time of the season as players become increasingly dehydrated in the unfamiliar heat.

The second half seemed to follow an almost identical pattern to the first with Leeds building a supposedly match-winning lead before surrendering it and, but for a last-ditch tackle by Vince Fawcett, almost throwing the game away. Instead of sticking to the basic simple ploys for the full eighty minutes which had proved to be working we had developed a tendency to relax our concentration once we had got fourteen or sixteen points ahead with the players attempting their own individual forays instead. That frequently allowed the opposition back into the game and what should have been a comfortable victory again became a desperate affair. Despite the points glut, it was important to get our first victory since the semi-final shambles and to maintain our impressive home record which enabled us to be in a good position to launch an assault on the top four in the remaining run in.

Having become accustomed to almost continuous year-round rugby I did not appreciate a break at one of the most important times of the season. I became totally bored sitting around the house, especially as I was normally such an active person, and I am sure that I must have been difficult to live with whilst getting under the feet of the family. I felt the frustration most during the time when the rest of the boys were training together whilst I had to be content with keeping fit by coaching a local pub side instead. With time on my hands I found it difficult to avoid the constant rumours that resurfaced regarding my immediate future. One story doing the rounds was that I had been suspended after having been seen training at Castleford prior to being appointed as their player-coach. If I had believed all that was being written then my left arm was going to

159

Halifax, my right arm to Castleford, my left leg was rejoining Hull whilst my right one was staying with Leeds. The stories were turning up with such regularity that after a while I was able to laugh them off.

My wife went instead of me to the Alliance Cup Final at Headingley between Leeds and Wigan on the Thursday evening and from her reports it appeared to be a similar scenario to the first team, with our reserves holding out gamely for about fifty minutes before capitulating to a very powerful all-conquering side. The margin may well have flattered Wigan but their tactics of playing disciplined pressure football had obviously infiltrated at every level and had again paid off. The next day I received a letter from Headingley asking me to attend a meeting on completion of my suspension in Doug Laughton's office at 2.30 the following Monday afternoon for a general discussion.

Great Britain v France - British Coal Test 2/4/93

The appointment of Wakefield coach, David Topliss, as a consultant to the French side when they arrived here to prepare them more thoroughly for the demands of modern Test match football seemed a good idea. His contribution to tightening their defensive strategies and improving their attacking organisation would have been welcomed but was never likely to affect the result. The game was featured live on Sky Sports and full match commentary was carried nationally on BBC Radio 5, allowing the code the right sort of recognition and exposure it deserved at international level. The main talking point before the game was the late axing of Ellery Hanley from the line up for apparently leaving the Great Britain camp during the final preparations. This came out of the blue and mystified me when I heard it announced.

It was particularly hard watching the Great Britain team being led out on my home ground which was something that I had been keenly

160

anticipating. I sang the national anthem along with them from my lounge armchair which was difficult enough but I felt even worse when my son asked me why I was not out there with them. It was hard to explain to a three-year-old what the truth was especially as he normally liked to go along and watch. The nearest I could get to the action was to be with the team in spirit. Right from the beginning of the match the obvious disparity in power between the sides was again evident as the rampant British forwards ran riot. It appeared that Malcolm Reilly had drilled into the side the need not to let the French off the hook and he must have gained great pleasure from the way they were systematically torn apart in a display of pace and power that had no answer. The creative skills illustrated the best aspects of the British game and the disciplined, ruthless defence would have severely tested either of the Antipodean sides. Perhaps most significantly, the lads kept their enthusiasm going throughout the entire match and gave meaning to an encounter that was otherwise in danger of becoming too easy to be useful. The ever-increasing score line fully justified Malcolm's selection policy of picking his strongest side available, getting the best result, and allowing it to gel together in readiness for the impending clashes with the Kiwis. The blend and balance seemed right with some fierce heavyweight pack performances marshalled by Shaun Edwards and Jonathan Davies at half back. They also brought the best out of the centre combination of Gary Connolly and Man of the Match Paul Newlove who themselves combined well with the pace on the flanks and from Alan Tait at fullback.

The enterprising decision by the Rugby League Headquarters to distribute free tickets to local school children also paid off as the crowd exceeded expectations and generated a vibrant atmosphere. They must have enjoyed the entertaining exhibition of their heroes and the team would certainly have appreciated their response and support. The outcome of a world record Test match victory offered tremendous scope for positive publicity in the aftermatch reports and even the Aussies would have taken notice of the result which reflected great credit on all those associated with it. My biggest regret was not that I had missed being part of the history making extravaganza, but the fact that I had again foregone a domestic honour when Andy Platt lifted the British Coal Trophy. It was nice of him to mention in his post match interview that whilst he had enjoyed the captaincy he hoped it would only be a temporary appointment until my eventual return. Much of the talk afterwards centred on how we could offer our support to help the French rebuild their game. The onus must really be on them first and foremost to put their own house in order and to employ the methods required to match our advancement. I doubted that we would see anything of them if the boot had been on the other foot.

Saint Helens (Away) - Stones Bitter Championship 4/4/93

Sunday afternoon again found me in the unaccustomed position of following Leeds' fortunes on the radio. Although my ban did not extend to away grounds, it would not have been appreciated if I had turned up and I did not want to jeopardise my position. The match marked our last direct influence on the outcome of the Championship and we were determined to spoil Saints' prospects and enhance our own top four claims and credibility. It sounded like a positive start and our defence held firm for the initial quarter before we again proved to ourselves that you cannot make mistakes at this level without being severely punished. Four errors were all turned into tries and all of a sudden there was a mountain left to climb with a large interval deficit. The defensive pattern generally seemed quite good in spite of individual errors but again the resilience shown after the break was finally undermined by a dropped ball which saw Alan Hunte register a long distance try and the floodgates opened. Amazingly, we had held Saints scoreless for about fifty minutes in total which meant that they racked up their forty-two points in only half an hour which set the alarm bells ringing. The late collapse was further evidence that our concentration levels were still lacking and that detracted from any amount of honest endeavour. I was quite disillusioned by the final margin as the relatively infrequent score flashes, reports and commentary had not indicated such a heavy defeat was likely. It was impossible to assess the performance and the reasons for it until reading Trevor Watson's more comprehensive and considered report in the *Yorkshire Evening Post* the next day which again highlighted our self-destruct capability.

Chapter Fifteen

Back in the Fold

With my suspension completed, I returned to the club at the appointed time for my meeting with team manager Doug Laughton. I had not really planned what I was going to say or tried to rationalise what might have been on the agenda but it soon became clear that we were both in agreement that the best way forward was to look ahead and start afresh rather than go over old ground. Doug asked me how I thought the other players were going to react when I attended training the next day and when I told him that I did not really know he gave me the very valuable advice that I should consider apologizing to them for letting them down and to stress that we all needed to pull together if we were to make the final of the Premiership play-offs. I felt that the frank discussions had cleared the air but unfortunately I was then struck down by 'flu which I caught from the kids, and when I rang the physio to report in sick on the Tuesday morning I was extremely conscious of what people would be thinking. I phoned Doug the next day to inform him that I needed a further twenty-four hours to shake off the effects and he agreed that it would be unwise to come back too quickly and risk spreading the virus around the dressing room.

With the traditional Good Friday night match looming, I had not been left much time for preparation but I was raring to go when I finally attended training on the Thursday. After a couple of warm up laps I called the rest of the squad together and said my piece which I felt they appreciated as I got a very positive feedback from them. The overall mood seemed to be one of renewed determination towards the remainder of the season and I sensed that we had finally rid ourselves of the semi-final spectre. We knew that our credibility was still on the line but we were confident of beating Leigh despite their improved standing and efforts under the direction of new coach Steve Simms. We were all looking forward to a sound and solid home performance.

Before that, the producer of BBC's *Grandstand* programme, Malcolm Kemp, rang me to ask if I would act as the studio guest during their coverage of the Silk Cut Challenge Cup Final. I was delighted as it represented a vital role in projecting the code to a massive audience some of whom only tuned in once a year for the game's big day. I had occupied the same chair the year before and marvelled at the coolness of presenter Steve Rider under extreme pressure and had really enjoyed it. Despite being nervous first time around, my performance must have impressed them enough to ask me back and I regarded the invitation as an honour which I was very pleased to accept. However, nothing can compare to playing at such an illustrious venue on a prestigious occasion.

At around the same time, Leeds decided to engage the services of top Australian fitness conditioner, Bob Lannigan, to supervise the pre-season training programme although that was unknown by most of the players. I had heard nothing about it but knew of him from his work with Wigan and the Kangaroo Test team. He obviously had a great reputation and would bring a few good innovative ideas with him. I was passed fit for the encounter with Leigh and was pleased to have been selected especially in my usual position of stand-off but unfortunately the game was called off in the late afternoon because of a water-logged pitch at Headingley after nearly a week of incessant rain. I could not recall that ever having happened before during my time in the game and I had been looking forward to the run out as I had not played for five weeks and was desperate for some match practice prior to the big Easter Monday clash at Castleford. No amount of training could be a substitute for full match fitness and the only way to regain it was through the rigours of playing. I was told by phone at 4.30, three hours prior to the scheduled kick off and it came as a great and unwelcome surprise as by then I was already in the midst of my mental and physical preparations. I had been trying to relax during the day, had restricted myself to just two oranges for breakfast and a couple more for lunch and had just woken up from a light nap and was thinking about the game ahead. I would still have preferred to turn out even if the match had been played on a heavy pitch with standing water, which would have suited Leigh as they had shown in our meeting at Hilton Park. The unexpected night off gave me the chance to follow Wigan and Saints on Sky which was being billed as the title decider, but with Leeds not being affected by the eventual outcome and the game involving two Lancashire clubs, I did not pay too much attention to it.

The postponement of the Leigh fixture and its subsequent rearrangement for the following Thursday evening meant that our training schedule was altered and we had to go in at eleven o'clock on the Sunday morning. That delayed my attendance as the guest of honour at the Women's Amateur Rugby League Cup Finals which were staged at Lawkholme Lane, Keighley. I went along with Lee Crooks who was giving his moral support to the Redhill Ladies' team from the Castleford area in their battle with the Wakefield Panthers and even going there with an open mind I honestly did not know what to expect. The standard of football and the passionate fervour both on and off the pitch caught me completely unawares. The handling and more especially the tackling were excellent and I thoroughly enjoyed the game which left a tremendous impression on me. I said at the presentation afterwards that if I could do any promotional work to aid their development that I would do so in an effort to get their game taken seriously as I had been enthralled by it. The whole afternoon really illustrated the true grass roots essence of the sport and I was amazed to find that all the women's teams from around the country had turned up to offer their vociferous support. The occasion was a credit to them all and I am sure that they enjoyed a good night afterwards. Their hosts, Keighley, had just completed a marvellous season themselves having won the last ever Third Division Championship a couple of days before and their Chairman, Mike Smith, and his Co-Director, Mike O'Neill, were at pains to point out to me the ambitious plans to develop the ground and team in a concerted attempt to bring about First Division football there. If their avowed intention to bring a few big name class players to the club succeeds then they could well be a force to be reckoned with in the years to come.

Castleford (Away) - Stones Bitter Championship 12/4/93

Wheldon Road is a very compact ground with cramped dressing-rooms and is not one that I usually enjoy going to. The crowd are right on top of the players and the pitch in late season was normally rock hard. I had asked Lee the day before if I would be able to wear moulded boots but he told me that it was very grassy and liable to be heavy going. I was worried that the under foot conditions would highlight my lack of stamina and I mentioned to our centres, Craig Innes and Kevin Iro, that if I needed a breather to regain a second wind that they would have to be ready to cover for me at stand-off. We listened to the heavy thunder storm that began about an hour before the kick off whilst we were getting changed and promptly decided to cancel our planned warm up on the pitch. When we did eventually come out the thunder was still echoing around the ground and the lightning flashing overhead which, although it seemed an appropriate backdrop for a fierce local derby, caused several anxious glances from some of the players.

I renewed my partnership with youngster Gareth Stephens and we again seemed to work quite well together as we both understand each other's strengths and seem to have complementary styles of play. We opened very impressively and managed to pin Castleford deep in their own half straight from the kick off. We knew that in their previous home match they had beaten Wigan with a very strong all round performance and we were determined to impose ourselves on them right from the start. Unlike some of our previous recent displays, we respected possession, used the ball well for each set of six tackles and managed to keep our error rate to a minimum. Our commitment to keeping the ball alive in spite of the conditions began to pay dividends as we started to create chances. The defensive concentration never let up and we were all working well for each other. Inevitably, our pressure football finally told and we posted a couple of tries in quick succession to put daylight between the sides. Castleford played their usual very condensed sliding defensive system but we countered it by managing to get outside them and then quickly switching the ball back inside. I was pleased to have been involved with the creation of the scores especially after my absence. We should have had a third try soon afterwards when Ellery carried on a great break from Alan Tait and floated the ball to me on the overlap and I dropped it behind me. Instead of allowing the play to continue, the referee blew for a knock on. If we had scored then it would effectively have killed off the contest but Castleford rallied prior to the break although we held firm.

Our interval lead, achieved up the hill, was encouraging and we knew that if we could maintain our discipline and continue to command possession then we would win, particularly as Castleford had played in a gruelling match at Wakefield on the previous Friday whereas we were still fresh. The Leeds forwards continued to maintain their dominance as a unit and they shared out the work load in the second half by taking it in turns to drive the ball in and drop each other off with switch passes in an effort to continually break the advantage line. The only real criticism was that for all our territorial supremacy we failed to trouble the scoreboard operator but we remained patient and disciplined. Even after we had conceded a try from a rare spilled ball, we knew that we were still in control despite a slender lead and a likely tense finish. If anything we responded the better and snuffed out the Castleford threat with a good kick and chase game that kept them in their own half. I had a spell covering at scrum half which I did not mind in open play but I am always a bit wary about how to feed the scrum, especially with the lax interpretation of what constitutes a fair strike. I had learnt from experience a couple of years before when I had been forced to play there for the first time in my career after David Cruikshank had been sent off in a game against Saint Helens at Headingley. That day I had fed the ball straight down the middle and we had lost two consecutive heels against the head after which our hooker Colin Maskill left me in no doubt as to what was required. Ever since then I have deliberately put the ball directly into the second row and risked being penalised for guaranteeing possession.

By the end of the match I hardly had enough energy to celebrate our hard-earned victory which kept the season alive and my shoulders, back and legs were still aching three or four days afterwards. We had again shown what we could do against one of the better sides if we stuck to the designated plan. There was never any doubt that we would score points with the calibre of players in the side but we had to combine that with the need to work for the right openings rather than be over-elaborate in the wrong part of the field. Our defensive display over the full eighty minutes gave us tremendous satisfaction and seemed to galvanise the team and our magnificent following for the final push for a top four place and a home Premiership tie. I heard some comments from the supporters afterwards that, whilst the team would have to go some way to wipe out the memory of our dismal showing at Central Park, a season's treble over Castleford had helped to lessen the gloom. Bearing in mind that I had been out of the game for a while I was relatively pleased with my own contribution which had been effective rather than spectacular. I felt that I could have done a bit more with the quality possession we had in their quarter but overall there were few complaints.

The enforced rearrangement of the Leigh fixture for the Thursday night of the last week of the regular league programme meant that we were tending to play matches rather than train. We had the Tuesday off after the Castleford game and reported back on the Wednesday for a very light session comprising mainly of practising a couple of defensive drills and some ball work which lasted for about forty-five minutes. The manner of the victory over Cas had given everyone a massive boost and by then the position regarding the top four was becoming clearer and our destiny was in our own hands. We knew that we would have to try and beat Leigh by a wide margin to enable us to overtake our great rivals, Bradford, whom we were due to face in the last game but the need for points did not alter our tactics or influence the team selection. I returned to my original position of centre because of an injury to Kevin Iro and to accommodate Graham Holroyd which I did not mind, it seemed to be the logical option as Carl Gibson and Vince Fawcett were nursing long term injuries and the Alliance Team had their own fixture backlog to overcome. Despite three years at stand-off in the heat of the action, it was not difficult to adapt to a role wider out for which I felt I was still suited. I had not forgotten the script and the switch enabled me to have my first good look at "Holly" in a half-back pairing with Gareth Stephens which was a glimpse into the future. Both of them are very quiet personalities and I mentioned to Doug that I would try and call the shots from out in the centres to alleviate the pressure on the young lads and to help them when worrying about how to dictate to the more experienced professionals around them. Even though the match marked my return to action at Headingley since the semi and the ban, I was not particularly worried about what the crowd reaction might be. I knew what to expect, especially as my wife had already heard various

171

Keeping Peter Coyne occupied. *(Credit - Andy Howard)*

Determined to keep going despite the lay off. *(Credit - Andy Howard)*

comments being made about me in some sections and the only real reply could be on the pitch doing the job required to the best of my ability.

Leigh (Home) - Stones Bitter Championship 15/4/93

Having recovered from a horrendous start to the season, our opponents had nothing to lose as they ran out at Headingley. They knew that they could not be relegated but to their credit they were still determined not to end up in one of the bottom two places and had a lot of emerging juniors in the side who would have relished the chance to play on the wide open spaces. In contrast, the atmosphere in our dressing-room seemed a bit flat and there was an almost dangerous air about the place that all we had to do was to turn out to win. That attitude seemed to be matched by the supporters and the commendable crowd for a match being played on an unusual mid-week night also seemed a little muted during our warm up.

Leigh, who had been given a new tactical direction and defensive rigidity by their rookie Australian coach, Steve Simms, started out with all guns blazing in an attempt to grind us down. It was as if it was a relief for them to leave behind their tribulations over the uncertainty regarding the future of their own ground at Hilton Park which threatened their survival. I was opposing a player about whom I knew nothing, an Aussie called Dean Hanger. I later heard that he had been living for three or four months under John Monie's wing and training with Wigan before being released to Leigh as he was surplus to the Central Park quota. Beforehand I had asked around if he was built like the typical six foot three seventeen stone Australian centre as I had hoped I had got rid of them after confronting Mal Meninga in the World Cup Final. In the flesh, whilst he did not share their physique, he certainly had the talent to make a name for himself.

Both defences were generous early on, we conceded a try before we had even touched the ball and scored a long distance effort from our first real attack and from that passage we knew that we had to pick up our enthusiasm. I had to wait for about ten minutes before touching the ball, having spent the early period trying to marshal the play the ball moves and defensive line to repel Leigh's purposeful bursts and their ability to slip the ball away to the supporting players. Their enthusiasm was epitomised by their rugged prop Tim Street who perhaps had the added incentive of knowing that it had been heavily rumoured in the press that Leeds were interested in signing him for the following season. I moved infield on a sixth tackle option to help create a try for Jim Fallon but we were still only playing in short bursts rather than with concerted effort. The ploy of coming inside worked again when I set up first Ellery and then "Holly" for further tries and I received a good response from the crowd and was happy to acknowledge their chants.

The instructions at the interval centred on the need to shake off our lethargy and tighten the defence but having taken what should have been a decisive 28-14 lead we again fell way off the pace and nearly paid the penalty for a lack-lustre performance. Our seemingly inevitable mistakes gifted Leigh the tries that kept the scores close although the bizarre awarding of a penalty try against me by referee Robin Whitfield was strange to say the least. We were scampering back to cover a break from the base of the scrum by Leigh's Jason Donohue and when the ball was switched to Troy Clarke I let him run the required ten metres to put myself on side before bringing him down close to the line. Robin obviously thought that I had come from an offside position and told me as we jogged back to the centre spot that he had had no option but to award the try. If I had infringed I would have thought that the awarding of a penalty and even a sin-binning for a so-called professional foul would have been more appropriate and I remained mystified along with the majority of the crowd. Quite unbelievably, that was the only penalty he awarded during the entire match despite frequent calls for forward passes, high tackles, holding down and offside from the terraces but that is his particular trait in his desire to keep the game moving. It can, however, lead to great confusion amongst the players.

The glut of early points dried up in the final quarter which remained scoreless mainly due to our continued casual play. In the end, we were lucky to hang on for a victory which had been principally secured through Simon Irving's sure footedness. Afterwards, when we learnt that we would have to beat Bradford by over thirty points to overtake them and finish in the top four we knew that we would have to shake off our sluggishness if we were to compete seriously with the very best.

I was pretty shattered after the match but we had only two days to recover from the knocks before the usually explosive struggle with our fiercest rivals. The need to play three big games in six days was asking a lot of the human body which hardly had time to recover from the bruising. Doug put a foot note in his Friday column for the *Yorkshire Evening Post* commending me on the manner of my return and asked for the public and media to allow me to just go out and play rather than continue any speculation which was a sentiment that I fully endorsed and felt that it was a vital ingredient if we were to all be successful. That evening Sky screened Wigan's title decider at home to Castleford and I tried to phone Lee Crooks all through the day to offer him my support but the team had already left in order to maximize their preparations in the hope of spoiling Wigan's now customary celebrations. I was in total agreement with Castleford's scrum half Mike Ford who when interviewed prior to the match, stated that he did not want Wigan to win everything. It was, however, a fitting climax to the Championship that the destiny of the trophy had gone to the final week. Saint Helens' consistency in pushing Wigan all the way had at least given some hope to the other aspiring sides but I could not back their claims for a play-off if Wigan won the match which would have resulted in them claiming the prize by virtue of a

176

superior points difference. It is all very well pleading for an extra game when that sort of situation arises but the rules of the competition were set at its outset. Everybody knew what they were up against nine months beforehand and I believed that the format was the correct one. Wigan duly won the match courtesy of a scoring blitz at the beginning of the second half and despite a gallant late Castleford reply they deservedly took the spoils. The debates then began as to whether their continued success was good for the game but I had no doubts that they had earned their rewards and that the onus was on the rest of the teams to match them. No other side in the history of the game has equalled the consistency of their achievements over the last seven or eight years and I do not think that anyone ever will. To go to Wembley six times on the trot and hold the Championship for four consecutive years is a quite remarkable achievement. They have to go down as the best squad there has ever been and a credit to coaches Graham Lowe and his successor and surpasser John Monie. The gap may well be closing slowly between Wigan and the contenders for their mantle but anyone who assumes that, just because there will be a change in coach and player personnel at Central Park they will automatically come off the rails is deluding themselves. Wigan will continue to come good at the business end of the season when it really matters.

Our match with Bradford was our last guaranteed home encounter of the season and even though we knew we needed a huge points swing our only concern was to secure a victory. If we had put the added pressure on ourselves to try to achieve the thirty-two point margin required then we would have been dropping passes all over the park as we attempted to force an unrealistic pace. More importantly for myself and the team as a whole, we wanted to avenge our humiliating away defeat against them and hopefully to wipe out the memory of possibly our worst team display of the entire campaign. Before the game it looked realistic that the sides would be meeting again at Odsal the following week in the first round of the Premiership and we were geared up for gaining an important psychological advantage if that was the case. I was back at stand-off and our latest acquisition from Rugby Union, teenage winger Jonathan Scales, was on début as Craig Innes had lost his fifteen month ever-present run through injury which greatly disappointed him. I had not met Jonathan before he was drafted into the training session on the Saturday morning but he was gaining a growing reputation in the Alliance side for being quick and strong.

Bradford Northern (Home) - Stones Bitter Championship 18/4/93

The Headingley pitch, which had unusually come in for a bit of criticism during the year, was not in pristine condition in spite of the best efforts of the ground staff who had worked manfully to repair the divots caused by the Academy curtain raiser. At training it had been bone hard but the rain and wind leading up to the match did us a favour. I had hoped to be opposing Neil Summers to get revenge for our earlier meeting but he had been switched to hooker and I found that I was up against one of the form players of the year, Kiwi international Dave Watson. I had enjoyed my previous tussles against him and hoped that this particular clash was going to be a forerunner for the autumn Test series. He is a live wire character and an awkward customer to mark with a good range of pace and skills and a physical dimension to his play. As Ellery tossed up I called the lads round to issue some last minute instructions and I stressed that even though it was the last league game of a long season that we still had everything to prove. We knew that we were facing the biggest and possibly toughest pack in the league which would prove a daunting challenge but after the early exchanges I felt that some of their players were carrying injuries and shying away from the more ferocious confrontations.

We achieved our initial aims of starting at a great pace so as to put

Bradford on the back foot and trying to constantly move their pack around, as we thought that we had the edge up front in mobility. We gained momentum and territorial supremacy from our quick play the balls, hounded them into errors and mopped up all the loose balls. Our tactics to play a little wider out in an effort to find some more room to launch our backs seemed to work and our centres Simon Irving and Kevin Iro ran some good angles. I also knew that I had to get a bit deeper in order to counter the targeted crash tackles favoured by Paul Medley of which I had previously been on the receiving end. Before we eventually took the lead with a penalty, we had bombed tries on each wing with the final passes just going astray but we took heart from the fact that we were creating quality chances especially from moves using the blind side. We had worked hard on that ploy over the previous few weeks and it was proving effective, especially when we switched the ball quickly to a full set back line.

Even though we had dominated the first period, we were not worried that we only had a slender lead to show for our endeavours because we knew that scoring opportunities were there. We were reliant on our forwards continuing to make regular bursts and the hard yards over the gain line as we were facing a strong wind. Fortunately, they carried on where they had left off with some tremendous charges that enabled us to put in an effective kicking game that tied Northern down. We were helped by a magnificent try on the restart when Alan Tait stripped the cover for pace when latching on to a break by Ellery off the ruck. That got everything moving in the right direction and the whole side responded. Bradford were forced to reshuffle and I found myself briefly confronting the guile of Neil Summers which I relished and even though they appeared to be a bit laboured in their approach work, we allowed them back into the game. I was the culprit with a diabolical free kick that failed to find touch. That aspect is something that I practise regularly in training and on that occasion I was trying to be too greedy from a tight angle and went for distance instead of safety. I held my hands up to the lads as we regrouped behind the posts and promised to make it up to them at the other end. We did respond almost immediately to get Jim Fallon over and then missed a further chance to extend the lead when Simon Irving was caught in the corner. Almost from the restart we stood off in a tackle and Bradford broke from their own twenty-five to draw level.

The tension began to increase and culminated in a couple of sin-binnings after my old Leeds colleague Dave Heron had used a forearm to halt Gary Mercer's progress. James Lowes took exception and when I pulled David away I tried to advise him that such a hot headed action was not part of his game and that he was getting too old for that kind of confrontation. I was switching between the half back positions and the temporary loss of two players created the extra space needed for us to seal the game with two late tries, the last one after my long pass had released Jim Fallon. The injury to Bradford centre Tony Marchant in the lead up looked serious when he left the field on a stretcher in a neck brace but we found out immediately afterwards from their physio that even though he had been taken straight to hospital it had only been as a precaution. The crowd certainly appreciated the victory and we were conscious that overall it had been a commendable performance against a reputable side although it had been obvious that Bradford's main attacking weapon, Deryck Fox, had not been fully fit and did not do himself justice. It was galling to lose out eventually on a top four spot on points difference especially as our attack had been comparable with the two Championship chasing sides. Our record in the second half of the season that had seen us gain eleven wins and a draw from fifteen games was also highly satisfactory but our inconsistencies and lack of concentration on defence, particularly away from home, had let us down. As the other results filtered through into the dressing-room it was confirmed that we had finished fifth despite being level on points with Bradford who had ended up third and that we would be travelling to Widnes in the Premiership. We were happy to be facing them in the week prior to their cup date at Wembley even though we knew that a few of their stars would be playing for their places on the big day. One of our major aims at the start of the season had been to be the best team in Yorkshire and we had managed to finish just behind but on the same mark as Bradford. Significantly for me, we were just above Castleford which meant that I was owed money by Lee Crooks and that I could spend the next twelve months reminding him about it. We had ended up in exactly the same final placing as the previous year so it was difficult to assess what progress we had made. We knew that on our day we were a very good side and capable of matching the best but that we had to turn that into the rule rather than the exception if we were to achieve the silverware that we longed for.

On the look out for Dave Watson. *(Credit - Peter Heston)*

Searching for a gap. *(Credit - Peter Heston)*

Chapter Sixteen

Last Chance for Glory

The cumulative effect of four consecutive league wins was that we finished the regular season on something of a high and were justifiably confident about progressing in the top eight Premiership play-offs and reaching the prestigious finals day at Old Trafford. The trip to Naughton Park in the first round gave us an early opportunity to avenge our Challenge Cup humiliation and we were very eager for the contest. Much has been made of the curse of "Wembleyitis" that seems to effect most teams once they have qualified for the showpiece occasion and causes their form to dip as players hold back from full scale confrontation during the lead up, in an effort to remain injury-free. If we had allowed ourselves to believe that Widnes would be approaching this tie in that manner, then we would have been in danger of suffering an early exit and the need to be on top form was constantly emphasised during training. I was relishing the chance of another personal duel with Jonathan Davies and was determined not to allow him and Bobby Goulding to get the upper hand and dictate matters.

On the Thursday evening, the first of the annual end of season presentation nights took place as the Alliance players gathered to honour the winner of the Chris Sanderson Memorial Trophy for their outstanding performer of the season. It was a shame that only myself and Colin Maskill from the senior squad attended and saw David Creasser present it to promising newcomer Lee Harland. For any such event it is important that all the playing, coaching and backroom staff are present to offer their support and encouragement in an attempt to foster a genuine family spirit. That sort of backing gives everyone a big lift and makes them feel an integral part of the club.

Widnes (Away) - Stones Bitter Premiership 25/4/93

Despite the heavy conditions and persistent rain leading up to the game, we were determined not to let it degenerate into a forwards' battle. We had allowed that to happen in the semi and been overwhelmed and we knew that we had to stand back a bit and attempt to unsettle their bigger pack. We had a distinct advantage in the centres where Widnes' selection of David Hulme out of his normal position in an effort to snuff out the threat of Kevin Iro was certainly a negative tactic and one that we intended to exploit. The way that Widnes started the match showed that any thoughts of the following weekend were furthermost from their minds as they really got stuck into us. The early play from both sides was characterised by mistakes when in possession but any continuity was interrupted by a stream of penalties that served to stamp the referee's authority on the proceedings but tended to disrupt the flow.

We anticipated that if we could hold the Chemics for the first twenty minutes then they might start easing off and we would take over but they showed no signs of slackening and kept knocking us about. For the most part our defence was solid and I had to be heavily involved as a lot of the play was contained in the middle of the park. A sweeping length of the field try to give them the lead kept us on our guard and Ellery's harsh words of warning behind the sticks left us in no doubt as to what was required. Unusually, the broken play kickers on both sides were having their efforts frequently charged down as both defensive lines were extremely well drilled at moving up into the opposition ranks and it was noted at half-time that if that facet of our game was to be more effective at putting them under pressure then Andy Gregory and I needed to readjust our positioning accordingly. When the ball was in our hands, our midfield combination work and close support play improved as the half progressed but at half-time Dougie instructed Andy and me to run at our opposite numbers more often and to look to take them on rather than just off-load a pass without committing the defender first. We had proved with Simon Irving's try prior to the interval that if we positioned our supports into the gaps we would take some holding. That we did not go in with the lead was again due to some slack marking; the hooter was about to sound after we had surrendered about sixty yards on the intervention of a touch judge who penalised us twice in succession to give Widnes the platform to go over in the corner.

The first opening that we carved out after the restart saw us regain the lead after I supported an incisive break from Alan Tait for a try between the posts. I was quietly satisfied at having got amongst the scorers again and was pleased with the crowd's ecstatic response and reaction which I really appreciated. From then on we consolidated and prevented Widnes from playing their usual flamboyant football and they never really looked like scoring again. By then, injuries had taken their toll and having used their substitutes early on, they struggled to regroup and started to leave gaps which we systematically exploited. Both of our prop forwards set the lead with Steve Molloy anxious to put his display in the semi behind him and keeping going forward all afternoon and Paul Dixon always dangerous when charging into the opposing pack and almost defying them to hold him. We took a while finally to accept our chances as again we were guilty of trying to put in one pass too many whenever we made a clean break. Fortunately, our defence around the ruck area more than compensated in what was probably our most effective forty minutes away all season and

187

we knew that once we had won back the lead we could maintain the advantage. Widnes have changed their style under Phil Larder and follow a more rigid Australian inspired doctrine of holding the ball for four or five tackles before putting in a deep kick and chase and trying to promote a mistake. We managed to cut out our unforced errors and finally killed the game off with two late tries after some impressive handling.

Our performance certainly answered some of the critics and proved that in the right frame of mind we could come through the stiffest of tests. It left our supporters quite naturally wondering why we had not come up with such a professional display when it had really mattered. The victory meant a trip to Saint Helens in the Premiership semi-final and having seen them struggle to overcome Halifax on the Friday night, we were sure that they were beatable. Our best side was available for selection although even after playing five games in thirteen days which had brought me back nearer to full fitness, I was not overjoyed with my own form and felt that I could improve, especially with regard to the creation of quality openings for the back row.

Even though the clash with Saints could not come soon enough for us we had to wait a fortnight to accommodate the Challenge Cup Final which rightly took pride of place the next weekend. Dougie left us in no doubt right from the outset that he was going to work us hard in the interim as he believed that fitness and stamina were going to be the key factors for success. Anyone watching the sessions would have thought that we were already doing our pre-season work. We trained daily, had the Saturday off for Wembley and were back in on the Sunday afternoon at four o'clock and so hardly had time to notice the wait between rounds. Being another semi-final, it was important for us to be mentally and psychologically right if we were to break through that last minute hurdle but talk in the dressing-room centred mainly on trying to dovetail our individual roles into a collective effort.

The spate of entertaining social obligations and invitations was beginning to gather momentum and on the Monday night I was the Guest of Honour at the Yorkshire Executive Sporting Club's Boxing Dinner at the Norfolk Gardens Hotel in Bradford. On my arrival, I was astonished to find when I checked the menu that I was the chief speaker and had been earmarked for my début on the after dinner circuit. I had been surprised initially when organiser Wally Springett had informed me and my guests, Simon Irving and Paul Dixon, that we were all on the top table. In the audience were several of Leeds United's finest players, including David Batty, Tony Dorigo, David Rocastle, Chris Whyte and the Wallace twins as well as Paul Jarvis, the Yorkshire and England cricketer and we were a little embarrassed and overawed that we had been fêted in front of such illustrious company. I checked with compère John Morgan if I was required to say a few words especially as rather disconcertingly I was listed above the comedian in the running order. I quickly wrote a few notes, mainly welcoming the other celebrities and remembering a few choice incidents and anecdotes from the recent tour but by the time my turn came round and the introductions had been made, I had thrown them away as all my best lines had already been used. I was forced to ad lib and was up there for about ten or fifteen minutes, terrified by the whole experience. The night as a whole was excellent and the boxing quite good even though I am not a fan of the sport. There are marginally more punches thrown in the ring than in an average Rugby League encounter.

As we got into the intensive training schedule comparisons were inevitably drawn with our performance against Wigan at a similar stage the previous season. We had gone into that game assuming that our opponents would not be bothered about winning the prize having just retained the league and cup double and returned victorious from Wembley for the then fifth successive year. As it turned out, we learnt the hard way by suffering our worst ever defeat and were determined to be properly prepared this time around. Dougie was convinced that it would be a hot day and that conditioning was vital and with Saints having run Wigan so close in all the other competitions but come up empty handed, we knew that they would not be short of incentive. Some of our other commitments had to be postponed so as to accommodate the extra training demands, including for me the planned attendance at a kids' introduction day in Peterborough accompanying the Leeds Development Officer, Damien McGrath. I conveyed my apologies on this occasion having done a similar venture there before and National Development Officer, Tom O'Donnovan took my place instead. It was, therefore, very annoying to read in the next issue of *League Express* that I had let everyone down as that was never my intention and my absence was unavoidable. Their intimation that the episode had caused a further rift between Doug Laughton and myself was also totally wrong. I spend as much time as possible travelling round with Damien to wherever there is an interest in Rugby League and spreading the gospel to the kids, often at very short notice. We work very well together either coaching or doing presentations and the standard and enthusiasm certainly makes it rewarding. All the kids seem to want to have the ball in their hands and to run as far as they can with it and we try to give them some sort of structure relating to catching, passing and tackling to work around. As a consequence of changes in the education system, especially now that teachers do not get paid to cover extra-curricular activities, specific sports are becoming increasingly marginalised or removed altogether and this has taken away a lot of the kids' options. Their formal activities are now restricted mainly to P.E. time which often means a four week cycle of Rugby League, Soccer and Hockey in the winter which denies the pupils the chance to pursue their preference and interest. The onus is on everyone concerned about the code to help to look after its future.

Towards the end of the week, my attention turned to my impending appearance as an analyst on *Grandstand*. I went down with my wife on the Friday afternoon following training and arrived at the Kensington Park

Hotel at around six o'clock and got changed and ready for the sponsor's dinner hosted by Silk Cut for the Rugby League hierarchy and the media which was a great success. I did not prepare anything specific for the programme, my only instructions came from Sally Richardson at the BBC and that was to be at Wembley by 11.45. That caught me slightly unawares as I had not realised that I would be required at the opening of the show for the scene setting and it was quite a nerve wracking thought. I actually got to the stadium at 10.30 but there were no rehearsals or advanced planning of what I would say or which questions I would be asked. The conversation between Steve Rider and myself was completely ad libbed at the side of the pitch and although he is not an expert on the intricacies of the game, he knows how to put his guests at ease and does not embarrass them with silly questions. As the time came to "go live" the tempo and tension increased and I made sure that I did not look at myself on any of the monitors as with the slightest glance the nerves can overwhelm you and after that it is almost impossible to remain composed. The trick is to pretend that you are being casually interviewed without the cameras being present but it is not easy. Once the introductions were over, I was not required again until 1.00 p.m. for the match preview but was so busy signing autographs around the perimeter that I almost missed my cue to return. Once we were in the studio which was situated just to the left of the tunnel on the top level on a par with the Olympic Gallery, I was made to feel part of the team and even though the box was only small, there were about nine technicians in attendance. Not surprisingly, it got incredibly warm in there, particularly with the glare of the television spotlights when they were on. After a while I felt that I had fitted into the role required of me and I tried to remain lucid and not pause unduly or repeat myself, even though it was hard constantly to review and comment on the replays of incidents from our defeat in the semi final.

The first time it really hit me that we had been so close to being there ourselves was when the teams emerged to sample the atmosphere and conditions prior to getting changed. Wigan were the first to arrive, an hour and three quarters before the kick off. The Widnes lads followed about ten minutes later and I cast an envious glance as they surveyed the enormity of their achievement. The BBC studio provided an excellent vantage point for viewing all the ensuing events and there was also a bank of three televisions from which to gain an alternative perspective if preferred. I was again particularly impressed with the standard of the pre-match entertainment which encompassed the now traditional under-elevens match, dancing and flag waving troupes, the community singing and a great military band. Credit must go to David Howes for putting the marvellous package together which provided the ideal showcase to promote the sport in its best light and gave the fans great value for money. Even Steve Rider and the camera crew were all tremendously impressed by the display. The fact that the code had moved with the times and followed the American concept of really putting on an all-embracing spectacle was an indication that we are going in the right direction.

From a pundit's point of view the final itself was almost perfect, with an open start, plenty of incident to comment on and a close score line at the interval which made a review of the action easier. I had thought that Widnes would adopt a more open style in an effort to get the ball away from the ruck area at the second or third man out and their early try proved that theory and set the tone for an absorbing contest. I was very impressed by the positioning of young referee Russell Smith who was officiating in his first major match and he was in exactly the right place to award Richie Eyres' legitimate touch down when several in the stadium had thought that it had come from a double movement. By half time a lot of my prematch technical analysis and predictions had been seen to have been accurate although it was not until Ray French mentioned it in his commentary that I was aware of the fact. As I was inwardly patting myself on the back, it occurred to me that he had pinched all my lines. We were joined during the break by the captain of the Australian Cricket team, Allan Border, whom

192

I had met once before after our Third Test defeat in Brisbane during the previous summer. His instant recognition of me and inquiry as to my welfare was very gratifying and again showed how much the profile of the code was respected world wide. He is a big League fan as are a lot of the Cricket lads, an avid Broncos follower and, in common with a lot of others in basically non contact sports who like to view our game, he was amazed by the physical aspect and the relatively low injury rate. I did not get a chance to chat to him further off the air after his short stint as he rejoined the rest of his touring compatriots who were the guests of the Rugby League and had only just arrived in the country. I tentatively arranged to meet him during the Fourth Cricket Test at Headingley where I planned to tempt him to a few XXXXs in an effort to derail his assault on the Ashes and hopefully give the English lads an advantage.

The second half may have had less open play but it was equally as absorbing as the first and in the end, the game contained everything associated with the sport, both good and bad. If anything it confirmed what were Wigan's greatest assets and illustrated some of the perennial flaws in the Widnes temperament. As the game wore on, Wigan's ability to force their opponents into making crucial mistakes came more to the fore and they were always in control, patient and able to step up a gear when it was needed. Both defences were very strong throughout although as growing frustration crept into the Chemics' play it became a little too robust and led to the dismissal of Richie Eyres who should also have been joined by his colleague, Bobby Goulding. The two fouls in question certainly provided major talking points although I doubted if they marred the occasion. Russell Smith again did exactly the right thing in sending Richie off for his intent even if Martin Offiah may have played on the incident a little. My mate Bobby Goulding was more fortunate only to get a severe lecture for his impetuous high challenge. I had mentioned to him before the game that he would need to keep himself under control and to try and enjoy the day if he was to be effective and up to that point he had been Widnes' best player by far.

The day seemed very long and was mentally tiring but immensely enjoyable. I left the ground at 5.30 on the Rugby League chartered coach and in the evening went out for a Chinese meal with my wife. I felt extremely fortunate to have been doing work that gave such job satisfaction and I would like to think that some form of future role in the broadcast media might figure in my plans somewhere.

Having played Saint Helens three times during the campaign and lost them all, we were not short of motivation when we returned to training. The Premiership tie marked my first appearance of the season at Knowsley Road having missed out on the Regal and Championship encounters and I was raring to go. There is usually a terrific atmosphere there from the minute you get off the bus and are surrounded by autograph hunters through to emerging on the pitch and receiving a friendly reception. Naturally we knew that we were going there as underdogs and a lot of people were predicting that it would be a high scoring encounter in the sun as both sides were renowned for their attacking strengths.

Prior to that, on the Tuesday night the other main club awards were presented and the *Harry Falkingham Trophy* for the Supporters' Player of the Year and the *Beilby Management Award* for the Players' Player both went to the same recipient, Ellery Hanley. We trained a little later that day because Dougie wanted us all to attend although alcohol had been banned for the entire week and we were only permitted to stay for an hour between eight and nine. That was a shame for the organisers and fans and it would perhaps have been better to hold them after the season had finished. The choice was undoubtedly the correct one, Ellery had been the most consistent performer even when the side had not been playing well and scored an impressive thirty-four tries as well as possessing an awesome defence and excellent attitude. He had certainly answered in the best possible and most effective way the critics who had written him off after his injury troubles of the previous year. Having also won both awards in the past I could also vouch for how much the accolade meant. Most supporters are very shrewd judges and have a first rate appreciation and understanding of the game and the recognition from one's peers is also very heartening. Under David Ward we had voted our own Man of the Match after every game and the winner was drawn from that poll, whereas Doug conducted a secret ballot at the end of the regular season and announced the winner in the dressing-room just prior to the presentation.

Saint Helens (Away) - Stones Bitter Premiership 9/5/93

The only change to our previous semi-final routine was that this time we left from Headingley with the fans' good wishes cheering us off. By the time we ran out on the pitch, it seemed as though the season had come full circle in that we were facing the same opponents in similar balmy conditions and backed by a large, fanatical, vociferous support just as we had been at the start some nine months before. We were really keyed up and fancied our chances against a side who had seemed to falter in the previous weeks. I was opposing Kiwi Tea Ropati, one of the form stand-offs of the season and was eagerly looking forward to the challenge, having come across him both at club and international level a few times before. He is a different sort of player to the norm in that position, being very strong and powerful and more prepared to run over you than use a swerve or a sidestep.

The anticipated full-blooded start and frenetic pace led to handling mistakes as both sides tended to try and open out the play too quickly before setting the correct foundation. Despite forcing the passes, we were pleased with the way that we took the game to Saints and having started to create clear cut chances, luck seemed to desert us in the final moment.

On three separate occasions we looked certain scorers but were caught on the line, first when Ellery knocked on trying to take an awkward bouncing ball, then when he was bundled into touch after Paul Dixon and I had released him on the blind side and finally when David Lyon held up his opposite number Alan Tait as he was about to reach over the whitewash. Our extra conditioning and preparation certainly paid off with regard to our determined defensive effort and we knew that we would have no problem in lasting the pace. For their part, Saints worked very hard closing down our short side options which was an area that we had pinpointed as being one of their weaknesses and had planned to continually threaten. Once a game plan is set and the players know their respective duties within it, it is difficult to switch to something else quickly without everyone being at sixes and sevens.

The bookies would have offered long odds on the contest remaining scoreless at half-time especially as the action had been non stop. We were amazed that we were not in front but we knew that the longer that we held them out the more the pressure would be on the home side, particularly as their supporters were beginning to get restless and impatient. Unfortunately for us, they broke the deadlock with a fifty-seventh minute drop goal followed almost immediately by a swift try and we were the ones needing to play "catch-up" football. We were extremely disappointed with the manner in which we allowed Shane Cooper to score having been primed to be vigilant to his ploy of running across the pitch and then dummying to his supports near the line. We were heavily punished for our first defensive lapse although we were aware that we still had sufficient time to make amends. It was important to get in a quick reply and to try to play the game in their twenty-five and in our first incursion there from the restart tempers boiled over and we earned a kickable penalty from the resulting square up. The price for it was that we lost Ellery in the sin bin along with Bernard Dwyer whose initial challenge at the play the ball had been very petty and unnecessary. Saints' back row man, Sonny Nickle, waded in and yet somehow Ellery was deemed to have been culpable although he had not incited their over reactions.

Immediately afterwards as we stepped up the pressure the game was turned by a controversial decision when a touch judge disallowed a try by Jim Fallon when the corner flag was knocked over in the act of scoring. At the time I was not sure if he had scored but all the replays afterwards clearly showed that it was David Lyon with his last ditch attempt at a tackle who had dislodged the post. Whilst we reflected on the incident, Saints broke away for a good try and instead of being 7-6 behind and on the rampage we were 13-2 down and the game had slipped away from us. For the remaining ten minutes I moved up to loose forward which I see as my long term position in the side once Ellery has decided to call it a day and Graham Holroyd, who came on, is ready to fill the stand-off berth on a regular basis. It was a role that I had really enjoyed when I had played there a couple of times the season before in Ellery's absence and had relished the greater all round involvement. Whether I can play there at international level is another matter especially with Philip Clarke around and staking his claim. By then the game had degenerated into a series of stops and starts as the end of season frustration began to take over and the realisation of further semi-final failure dawned. There was little consolation that the margin flattered Saints and we could not believe that we had not posted a try despite such a good attacking performance. The total deflation in the dressing-room afterwards signalled that the season had drawn to an ignominious close and there was a tremendous feeling of anticlimax that all the hard work put in both pre and during the season had suddenly come to an end and come to nothing.

For some players there is little point in reflecting on what has passed and might have been, they prefer to look forward and anticipate instead.

There was no squad commemoration of the end of the campaign, just an instruction as to when to report back for arduous pre-season training. It was left to personal preference if anyone wanted to work on the weights or running before then as each player tends to know his own needs. Whilst it is vital to relax and recuperate, it is often difficult to adjust to the sudden freedom and release from routine. I attended the *Man of Steel Awards* in Manchester as a guest of the sponsors, Bass, and it was a fitting finale and tribute to and for the players which was very well received. The tremendous gala evening was carried live on Sky Sports for the first time and showed a different side to the popular conception of Rugby League players and stood on a par with all the other sporting ceremonies. We had a ten pound wager on our table as to who would win in each of the eight categories. I managed only two correct guesses and was surprised that Chris Joynt missed out on being crowned the best young player, that Russell Smith was not voted the premier referee and that John Monie was not made the 'Man of Steel' for his all round contribution to the game. If I had picked a composite form team of the year from those whom I had either played against or watched then it would have been:

1	Alan Tait
2	Jason Robinson
3	Gary Connolly
4	Paul Newlove
5	Alan Hunte
6	Frano Botica
7	Shaun Edwards
8	Lee Crooks
9	Martin Dermott
10	Andy Platt
11	Dennis Betts
12	Richie Eyres
13	Philip Clarke.

I doubt if that side would have lost many times and it would have been nice to have been the manager of it as I am sure that I would have struggled to have even got a place on the bench. I decided not to accept an invitation to attend the Premiership Final as I had had enough of going to events as a beaten semi-finalist. The day long format encompassing games at all levels has enhanced the competition and provides an excellent extravaganza for the fans of all clubs and projects a great image of the sport.

For the game as a whole, the season had been overshadowed by the events of "Black Wednesday" when a new structure had hurriedly been voted in and led to the expulsion of three member clubs from the fold and the game being seen as something of a laughing stock. Everyone knows that development takes time and structured planning and that if the code can emerge stronger as a unit then future efforts will stand a much greater chance of success. Internationally, the World Cup Final and its consequent promotional value proved to be a tremendous event as did the world record Test victory against the French. The overall standard of club football continued to improve and now stands us in good stead for taking on the might of first New Zealand and then Australia. If anything, an air of financial reality began to permeate the game again from the highest levels down to the individual clubs, although blaming the players' contract system for the economic problems served to deflect public opinion away from the real truth, that only club chairmen and directors know what resources are coming in and therefore what they can afford to pay their assets.

For Leeds, the obvious disappointment of not wining anything was tempered slightly by the fact that we had improved our home record, proved in patches that we could compete on equal terms with the best and reached two semi finals. If we can maintain the consistency achieved in mid-season then we know that we will be a force especially as the majority of the senior squad have now had time to integrate. Certainly there is no shortage of key people prepared to take on the hard work required although the call up of Kiwis Gary Mercer and Craig Innes for the summer Test series against the Aussies meant that they would miss the start of the pre-season build up when it is vital to get the team spirit going in order to meet the challenges ahead. Changes to the backroom staff following the departure of assistant coach, Gary Stephens, back to Halifax will no doubt bring new methods and ideas. As soon as the season finished there was a tremendous optimism about the place generated by the record season ticket sales and that level of support is tremendously inspiring and gratifying for all the staff.

Personally, it was hard to make sense of a year that had contained both career highlights and despairing lows. In truth, I was relieved to see the back of it and was looking forward to the next chance for glory. I finally entered hospital for my delayed ear operation and the extent of the damage was much more severe than anyone had previously anticipated. I was initially told to expect an hour and a half's surgery and a two day stay, but ended up being in theatre for over two hours and was kept in for four days. The persistent infection had led to a build up of different poisons inside and behind my ear and if I had delayed much longer then the consequences of a bang on the head or a gradual extension of it into the brain could have been life threatening. This came as a great shock when the doctor told me and in that respect at least I was glad that I had not gone to play for Manly during the summer. I then needed a second operation two weeks later to replace the internal dressing and packing hopefully to keep the infection at bay. The specialist estimated that the total course of treatment would take anything between three and four months and whilst that would undoubtedly affect my preparations I had already set myself a target of being available for selection for the first league game of the new season.

My final contribution to the 1992/3 season was to help organise a reunion dinner at Stoggy's in Leeds to celebrate the ten year anniversary of Hunslet Parkside Juniors winning the BARLA National Youth Cup. All the players, coaching and backroom staff were traced and invited along with some of the supporters who had accompanied us to Blackpool for the final and the vast majority turned up to reminisce about the fun we had had and to look back on those seemingly far off amateur days. It was an enormous success and went on well into the early hours as the stories got taller and the memories more blurred. At the time I had set myself goals and had expectations about what I might achieve in the professional game and if anyone had told me then that I would go on to be capped forty times and captain my country, gain selection on four tours and score over a hundred tries for two clubs then I would have been more than delighted and happy to retire on that alone.

Appendix

GARRY SCHOFIELD'S SEASON'S STATISTICS 1992-93

FOR LEEDS

ST. HELENS	(H)	CHAMPIONSHIP	L.14-27	1 TRY
HALIFAX	(A)	CHAMPIONSHIP	L.8-26	DID NOT SCORE
HUNSLET	(H)	YORKSHIRE CUP	W.28-20	1 TRY, 2 GOALS
HULL K.R.	(H)	CHAMPIONSHIP	W.34-6	1 TRY
HULL	(A)	YORKSHIRE CUP	L.16-26	1 TRY
BRADFORD N.	(A)	CHAMPIONSHIP	L.6-36	DID NOT SCORE
WARRINGTON	(H)	CHAMPIONSHIP	W.13-4	1 TRY, 1 DROP GOAL
WIGAN	(A)	CHAMPIONSHIP	L.6-24	1 TRY, 1 GOAL
WAKEFIELD T.	(A)	CHAMPIONSHIP	L.16-17	DID NOT PLAY*
WIDNES	(H)	CHAMPIONSHIP	W.48-16	8 GOALS
ST. HELENS	(A)	REGAL TROPHY	L.14-15	DID NOT PLAY**
HULL	(A)	CHAMPIONSHIP	L.19-22	DID NOT PLAY**
LEIGH	(A)	CHAMPIONSHIP	D.12-12	DID NOT SCORE
SHEFFIELD E.	(A)	CHAMPIONSHIP	L.14-31	DID NOT PLAY**
HALIFAX	(H)	CHAMPIONSHIP	W.42-14	5 GOALS
CASTLEFORD	(H)	CHAMPIONSHIP	W.40-12	1 TRY
SALFORD	(H)	CHAMPIONSHIP	W.38-14	DID NOT SCORE
WARRINGTON	(A)	CHAMPIONSHIP	W.31-24	2 TRIES, 1 GOAL 1 D. GOAL
SALFORD	(A)	CHAMPIONSHIP	W.46-15	DID NOT SCORE
BARROW	(H)	CHALLENGE CUP	W.54-18	1 TRY

HULL K.R.	(A)	CHAMPIONSHIP	W.18-16	DID NOT PLAY**
ROCHDALE	(H)	CHALLENGE CUP	W.68-6	3 TRIES
CASTLEFORD	(H)	CHALLENGE CUP	W.12-8	DID NOT SCORE
WIGAN	(H)	CHAMPIONSHIP	L.6-31	DID NOT SCORE
SHEFFIELD E.	(H)	CHAMPIONSHIP	W.46-10	DID NOT PLAY*
WIDNES	(N)	CHALLENGE CUP	L.4-39	DID NOT SCORE
WIDNES	(A)	CHAMPIONSHIP	L.8-19	DID NOT PLAY**
WAKEFIELD T.	(H)	CHAMPIONSHIP	D.26-26	DID NOT PLAY**
HULL	(H)	CHAMPIONSHIP	W.38-34	DID NOT PLAY***
ST. HELENS	(A)	CHAMPIONSHIP	L.8-42	DID NOT PLAY***
CASTLEFORD	(A)	CHAMPIONSHIP	W.10-6	DID NOT SCORE
LEIGH	(H)	CHAMPIONSHIP	W.28-26	DID NOT SCORE
BRADFORD N.	(H)	CHAMPIONSHIP	W.20-12	DID NOT SCORE
WIDNES	(A)	PREMIERSHIP	W.22-10	1 TRY
ST. HELENS	(A)	PREMIERSHIP	L.2-15	DID NOT SCORE

TOTAL   P.25/35   W.16/19   L.8/14   D.1/2   <u>TRIES</u> 14   <u>GOALS</u> 17   <u>D.GOALS</u> 2

FOR GREAT BRITAIN

AUSTRALIA	(H)	WORLD CUP FINAL	L.6-10	DID NOT SCORE
FRANCE	(A)	TEST MATCH	W.48-6	3 TRIES
FRANCE	(H)	TEST MATCH	W.72-6	DID NOT PLAY*

TOTAL   P.2/3   W.1/2   L.1/1   <u>TRIES</u> 3   <u>GOALS</u> 0   <u>D.GOALS</u> 0

FOR ENGLAND

WALES	(A)	INTERNATIONAL	W.36-11	1 TRY

TOTAL   P.1/1   W.1/1   <u>TRIES</u> 1   <u>GOALS</u> 0   <u>D.GOALS</u> 0

SEASON'S TOTAL   P.28   W.18   L.9   D.1   <u>TRIES</u> 18   <u>GOALS</u> 17   <u>D.GOALS</u> 2

*Ineligible   **Injured   ***Suspended